Wicklow County Council
County Library Services

KW-418-585

An Roinn Oideachais agus Eolaíochta
Department of Education and Science

Learning for Life:

White Paper on Adult Education

July 2000

BAILE ÁTHA CLIATH
ARNA FHOILSIÚ AG OIFIG AN tSOLÁTHAIR
Le Ceannach díreach ón
OIFIG DHÍOLTA FOILSEACHÁN RIALTAIS,
TEACH SUN ALLIANCE, SRÁID THEACH LAIGHEAN, BAILE ÁTHA CLIATH 2,
nó tríd an bpost ó
FOILSEACHÁIN RIALTAIS, AN RANNÓG POST-TRÁCHTA,
4-5 BÓTHAR FHEARCHAIR, BAILE ÁTHA CLIATH 2,
(Teil: 01 - 6613111 — fo-líne 4040/4045; fax: 01 - 4752760)
nó trí aon díoltóir leabhar.

———————————

DUBLIN
PUBLISHED BY THE STATIONERY OFFICE
To be purchased directly from the
GOVERNMENT PUBLICATIONS SALE OFFICE,
SUN ALLIANCE HOUSE, MOLESWORTH STREET, DUBLIN 2,
or by mail order from
GOVERNMENT PUBLICATIONS, POSTAL TRADE SECTION,
4 - 5 HARCOURT ROAD, DUBLIN 2,
(Tel: 01 - 6613111 — ext. 4040/4045; Fax: 01 - 4752760)
or through any bookseller

———————————

IR£ 5.00

Pn. 8840

© Government of Ireland

WICKLOW COUNTY COUNCIL

Date Recd 31/07/01

Inv. No. 5527

Acc. No. D18459

Class No. 374.9415 REE

Price £5.00

Contents

WICKLOW COUNTY COUNCIL

Date Recd 31/07/01

Inv. No. 5527

Acc. No. D18459

Class No. 374.9415 REE

Price £5.00

Contents

Page No

Foreword

The Green Paper: Adult Education in an Era of Lifelong Learning set out the role of adult education as a vital component in a continuum of lifelong learning. It outlined the contribution of the sector in promoting competitiveness and employment, addressing inter-generational poverty and disadvantage, strengthening individuals, families and communities, and promoting democracy and social cohesion. A major selling point in the new knowledge society is a well developed education and training system and a workforce which is adaptable and willing to learn new skills. Research throughout the world has demonstrated the central influence of education on life chances, and in recent years, there has been a growing realisation that education must be lifelong if we are to have an inclusive and democratic society which can adapt successfully to meet new challenges. In addition, we know that increasing childrenís participation and benefit from education is heavily dependent on also enabling parents to support their childrenís learning. Globalisation, increased competition, new technology, demographic change, a continuing need to upskill the workforce, more leisure time, and an emphasis on social and cultural development are all converging factors which make it an imperative to invest systematically in adult education.

The Green Paper set out the context for debate in this area and made recommendations on how the sector might evolve. Its publication was followed by a wide ranging consultation process with providers, funders, users, policy makers, research, social partner and community and voluntary sector interests. My thanks are due to all parties who contributed with expertise and enthusiasm to this process and whose contribution is helping to shape the future direction of our system.

A Lifelong Learning policy requires learning opportunities to be provided over a lifespan rather than only in the early years, a recognition that learning takes place in a wide variety of settings, the development of greater links with industry and other community services and between the formal and informal sectors, and ensuring that quality services are available to meet the diverse needs of a wide range of groups, both young and adult.

We are at the beginning of a new and exciting era. This White Paper sets out a blueprint for the future development and expansion of adult education, for a strengthened focus on access, quality, flexibility and responsiveness, and for the establishment of national and local structures which will help provide a co-ordinated and integrated approach. Adult Education is the last area of mass education which remains to be developed in Ireland. Many of the initial steps have already been taken and will be consolidated in the context of investment under the National Development Plan. This Paper provides for further development within the context of an over-arching policy and a comprehensive systemic approach. It will require the commitment and partnership of all – Government, education and training providers, business, trade unions, communities, voluntary organisations, individuals – to meet the challenge of bringing the concept of lifelong learning concept to reality.

Willie O Dea, T.D.
Minister of State

Department of Education and Science

Executive Summary

Executive Summary

RATIONALE AND CONTEXT

This is Ireland's first White Paper on Adult Education and marks the adoption of lifelong learning as the governing principle of educational policy. The Paper reflects on the role of adult education in society, builds on the consultation process following publication of the Green Paper, and sets out the Government's policies and priorities for the future development of the sector. It does not aim to provide a policy blueprint for the training sector given that this work is being advanced through the National Employment Action Plans and previous publications, and the work of the Task Force on Lifelong Learning recently established by the Department of Enterprise, Trade and Employment. Rather, it seeks to ensure that there is a fit and complementarity between education and training provision, so as to ensure that learners can move progressively and incrementally within an over-arching co-ordinated and learner-centred framework.

The Paper defines adult education as *"systematic learning undertaken by adults who return to learning having concluded initial education or training."* As such it includes aspects of further and third-level education, continuing education and training, community education, and other systematic deliberate learning by adults, both formal and informal. In setting out a role for adult education in society, six priority areas are identified:-

Consciousness Raising

Citizenship

Cohesion

Competitiveness

Cultural Development

Community Building

The Paper recommends that adult education should be underpinned by three core principles promoting:-

(a) **a systemic approach** which recognises that the interfaces between the different levels of educational provision, and the quality of the early school experience have a critical influence on learners' motivation and ability to access and progress in adult education and training. This requires that educational policies must de designed to embrace the life cycle, reflect the multiplicity of sites, both formal and informal, in which learning can take place, provide for appropriate supports such as guidance, counselling and childcare, and for mechanisms to assess learning independent of the context in which it occurs;

(b) **equality** of access, participation and outcome for participants in adult education, with pro-active strategies to counteract barriers arising from differences of socio-economic status, gender, ethnicity and disability. A key priority in promoting an inclusive society is to target investment towards those most at risk;

(c) **inter-culturalism** – the need to frame educational policy and practice in the context of serving a diverse population as opposed to a uniform one, and the development of curricula, materials, training and inservice, modes of assessment and delivery methods which accept such diversity as the norm. This refers not only to combating racism and encouraging participation of immigrants, refugees and asylum seekers in education, but also to a recognition that many minority groups such as travellers, people with disabilities, older adults, participants in disadvantaged areas may have distinct needs and cultural patterns which must be respected and reflected in an educational context. It also envisages a more active role by adult educators in the promotion of Irish language and culture.

Chapter 1 of the paper draws attention to emerging trends in participation in education, including the predominance of early school leaving among males, differences in subject options at second and third-level by gender, the inter-generational socio-economic influences on school participation and performance, poor educational levels of older adults in the population, comparatively high levels of the population scoring at the bottom literacy level, difficulties for women in accessing a range of active labour market programmes, and barriers such as access to childcare.

Chapters 2 and 3 set out the broad policy developments and reports which have occurred since the Green Paper was published which influence the context for adult education developments, and the feedback from the comprehensive consultation process which followed. While there was a widespread welcome for the Green Paper and its priorities and policy proposals, the main concerns voiced in the feedback were:-

• that the policy objectives for adult education should embrace personal, cultural and social goals as well as economic ones, and be seen as promoting collective as well as personal advancement;

• that issues of socio-economic status and gender, equality and inter-culturalism should underpin all adult education policy initiatives, with the needs of marginalised groups being identified and addressed explicitly, and with strategies to strengthen and expand the role of community education providers in this area;

• that barriers to access and progression arising from differentiated fee structures, accreditation difficulties, lack of flexibility and support services should be addressed. Almost all submissions stressed the urgency of developing flexible mechanisms for accreditation of prior and work-based learning;

- resounding criticisms of the proposals in the Green Paper to maintain the fee structure for part-time students in third-level education, and of proposals to charge fees for certain categories under the Back to Education Initiative. It was argued that this strategy would continue to discriminate against women in the home, and would present barriers to a return to learning for those with low skills and low educational levels in work.

- about local structures. There was widespread acceptance of the need for and the proposed role and functions of the National Adult Learning Council and the Local Adult Learning Boards, but little consensus regarding the hosting of the local structures. However, the level of attention given to this issue in the consultation process was less than expected, and where disagreement emerged, it crystallised around a pro-VEC or anti-VEC position.

PROPOSALS

The Government notes the prominence given in the consultation process to issues concerning free access for all to part-time adult education options under the Back to Education Initiative, and in relation to third-level education. However, at this stage, it is not considered feasible to introduce such an arrangement. Within the adult education sector itself there is a number of competing needs to be addressed. These include the need to significantly increase the scale and flexibility of existing provision, to promote strategic shifts towards adult-friendly policies within existing institutions, to invest systematically in the development of core supporting services such as guidance and counselling and childcare, and to provide for an increased role and funding for community education. Large scale increases in adult literacy investment, expansion of capital provision, implementation of an ICT programme for adults, specific equality initiatives to improve participation of marginalised groups, and structural developments are also needed. In addition, the number of adults in the population with low levels of education is simply too large for a general free access policy to be feasible. Given the scale of change needed, the Government's priority is to expand the flexibility and supply of core programmes and services for adults, and to concentrate fee relief on those most at risk. The impact of this policy will be monitored to assess the take-up by different target groups, particularly those with less than upper second-level education.

The Paper focuses on the adult learner in a number of key learning sites namely:-

School

Community

Workplace

Higher Education

FURTHER EDUCATION SCHOOLS AND CENTRES

In the Further Education sector, the recommendations provide for the development of a comprehensive framework for second-chance education for those with less than upper secondary education via:-

- **increased investment in adult literacy.** £73.6m is being provided under the National Development Plan to increase investment in this area, with a view to providing services over the lifetime of the Plan for some 110,000 adults. As part of the developments, a TV literacy awareness and tuition programme will be implemented to encourage a mass audience to access help and support;

- **a Back to Education Initiative** providing a major expansion of part-time options under PLC, Youthreach, and VTOS programmes, principally aimed at young people and adults in the population with less than upper secondary education. This will also provide for an increase in Foundation, Level 1, Leaving Certificate or equivalent options.

There will be **4 categories of beneficiary**:-

Youthreach/VTOS-eligible on full time courses. For full-time participants, there will be free tuition plus a training allowance or social welfare payment.

Other means-tested welfare payments, unemployment payments/Family Income Supplement recipients and their dependants, and VTOS/Youthreach eligible participants on part-time courses – free tuition will be provided but entitlement to continued welfare payments will be subject to their satisfying the Department of Social, Community and Family Affairs regarding the conditions of the relevant scheme (e.g. for instance, in the case of unemployment payments that the persons concerned are still actively available for and actively seeking work and that the course is likely to enchance their chances of gaaining a job). For Youthreach eligible participants attending part-time courses free tuition and a training allowance on a prorata basis may apply, to be funded by the Department of Education and Science.

Other unwaged participants with less than upper secondary education –
a reduction to 30% of tuition costs.

Remainder - people in this category will pay fees;

- an **adult ICT Basic Skills programme** will be included as part of the Back to Education Initiative;

- specific **capital provision** for the Further Education sector will be provided, to increase on a phased basis to at least £10m per annum;

- improved flexibility and organisational structures for **self-funded adult education** programmes;

- **a review of PLC management, organisational, administrative and technical support arrangements** to assess the appropriateness of existing structures to changing needs.

COMMUNITY EDUCATION

Community education, particularly in the form of community-based women's groups has been one of the most dynamic and distinctive elements of the Adult Education sector in recent years. Its self-directed, learner-centred character and its capacity to reach marginalised women in disadvantaged communities are particularly noteworthy. Its growth, however, has been constrained by a number of factors including:-

1. low levels of financial or other resource supports;

2. relative detachment from other elements of the education system, especially in areas such as assessment, accreditation and certification of the learning;

3. inadequate research support.

The Government now proposes to address these constraints by:-

- the appointment of **a national team of Community Education Facilitators** to be based in the Local Adult Learning Boards to support the development, maintenance and mainstreaming of such groups;

White Paper on Adult Education – Learning for Life

- exploring through this team of animateurs and through **central technical support from the National Adult Learning Council,** the approaches pioneered within the community-based women's groups to other sectors, specifically in relation to:-

    disadvantaged, hard-to-reach men;

    travellers and ethnic minorities;

    people with disability;

    community arts groups;

    the elderly;

- developing more streamlined, longer term and diverse funding channels to community education groups - **10% of all Back to Education Initiative increases in funding will be earmarked exclusively for community education**, in addition to the existing base under the Adult Literacy and Community Education Scheme. The community education sector will be one of the range of providers represented on local and national adult education structures;

- looking at a role for such groups in providing education and training services, particularly in disadvantaged communities on behalf of statutory bodies;

- promoting community arts both as an end in itself and as an accessible and powerful educational tool.

WORKPLACE EDUCATION

Skill shortages both in terms of new entrants to the workforce as well as the skills of those already in the workforce are now a major barrier to the sustainable development of the Irish economy. Both the *National Employment Action Plan (2000)* and the *National Development Plan (1999)* in recognising this, have now elevated lifelong learning to a pivotal role in labour market policy.

The central thrust of the proposals in this White Paper regarding workplace learning is the emergence of the workplace as a learning organisation committed to the ongoing development and empowerment of all its members. To support such a development, it is proposed to **encourage the development of partnerships/consortia of education/training and industry interests** along the lines of FIT, IBEC Business Education Links Scheme and European Orientation programmes advancing such issues as:-

- expanded industry and work placements in higher education institutions;

- agreements between education and industry on time-tabling and modularisation of course provision;

- recognition of work-based learning for accreditation purposes;

- delivery of courses in the workplace.

Flexible education and training options will be progressed, allied with a focus on **addressing barriers to participation** of those in the workplace in ongoing education and training, particularly those with the lowest skills. These issues will be addressed through the work of the recently established **Department of Enterprise, Trade and Employment Task Force on Lifelong Learning.**

A **working group** will be established to explore and cost the feasibility of treating all investment in education and training by employers on the same basis for **tax relief** purposes as other capital investment, and of providing tax relief for all participants for fees incurred in engaging in nationally certified learning programmes, irrespective of their location and duration

The National Qualifications Authority of Ireland will be asked to explore with the National Adult Learning Council the feasibility of a national training programme to establish a pool of highly skilled **Learning Assessors** to support mechanisms for the **accreditation of prior learning or work-based learning**.

The expansion of adult literacy services will include a focus on the development of **workplace literacy initiatives**

A **unit will be established within the National Adult Learning Council** to provide technical support and advice on initiatives and policies to promote education and training for those in the workplace.

HIGHER EDUCATION

The participation levels of mature students in Higher Education in Ireland is amongst the lowest in the OECD. The *Programme for Prosperity and Fairness 2000* sets a target for mature student representation in higher education - 15% by 2005.

To enable the realisation of this target it is now proposed to introduce **a targeted higher education mature student fund** which will increase on a phased basis to at least £10m per annum to enable third-level institutions to make innovative strategic shifts towards adult-friendly policies. The fund will be a competitive one to be disbursed on the basis of national criteria to institutions which display institution-wide directional shifts along the lines advocated in the Paper. Cross-faculty approaches, partnerships with other colleges, participation in networks to share results and mainstream good practice will be part of the requirements.

Fees will no longer apply to third-level part-time students who are means-tested social welfare or unemployment payment recipients or dependants, medical card holders or dependants, or Family Income Supplement holders or dependants and who are pursing first time under-graduate, nationally certified distance learning, or nationally certified certificate or diploma programmes (including university) or access programmes which guarantee entry.

SUPPORT SERVICES

The Government recognises that there are fundamental foundation blocks which must be put in place in building a comprehensive system of Adult Education within an overall framework of lifelong learning. In particular these include expanded provision for:-

- **Training of Trainers**— An **inter-agency Working Group** will be established to make recommendations **on the recognition of qualifications for adult education practitioners;**

- a **Forum of Adult Education Practitioners** – the National Adult Learning Council will be asked to establish such a forum in order to share good practice and input to policy developments;

- new approaches to assessment, accreditation and certification will be developed through the work of the of the **National Qualifications Authority of Ireland;**

- development of an **Educational Adult Guidance and Counselling service** on a phased basis. This will focus on improving and streamlining access to information, and developing a help-line service and ICT information points. Preliminary consultations with an advisor will be provided free to adults, with services also being put in place for more specialised counselling and assessment, and for referral to psychological services where needed. The full range of services will be free for participants on adult literacy, VTOS and Youthreach programmes, and to those entitled to fee remission or reduced charges under the Back to Education initiative, but the remaining categories will be charged fees for intensive follow-up consultations;

- **Research** – the National Adult Learning Council will incorporate a research role within its remit and will be given resources and staff for this purpose;

- **Childcare** – Additional funds will be provided under the National Development Plan to consolidate developments in childcare provision for VTOS, Youthreach and Traveller programmes, and to expand provision on a phased basis. This will be complemented by the £250m childcare programme under the National Development Plan being co-ordinated by the Department of Justice, Equality and Law Reform, and by the investments in the development of after-school services by the Department of Education and Science and the Department of Social, Community and Family Affairs.

The paper also includes a range of recommendations to promote increased access to mainstream adult education programmes for people with disabilities, Travellers, refugees and asylum seekers, and to address barriers in rural areas.

NORTHERN IRELAND

Cross border co-operation will, under the direction of the North/South Ministerial Council, build on the valuable linkages which have been developed to date, and promote inter-active approaches in Further and Higher Education in such areas as R&D support for small and medium sized enterprises, the development of lifelong learning, adult literacy and adult guidance and counselling programmes, information and communications technology in schools, and educational underachievement.

STRUCTURES

The White Paper proposes two layers in an over-arching structure for Adult Education – A National Adult Learning Council and, at local level, Local Adult Learning Boards.

The **National Adult Learning Council** will be established by the Minister for Education and Science as an Executive Agency of the Department to:-

- promote the co-ordinated development of adult education and training provision within an agreed national strategy and policy framework;

- to liaise with the wide variety of stakeholders in the field;

- to advise on quality standards and

- to engage in evaluation and research in the field of adult education.

The Council will also have a specific role in the funding, co-ordination and monitoring of programme and staff development initiatives for designated adult education programmes in the education sector.

The Council will have a governing body which will include representation from a broad range of interests including social partners, education and training providers, learners, community and voluntary pillar interests and the National Qualifications Authority of Ireland. The Council staff structure will have four broad units within it, focusing on Adult Education and the Formal Education Sector, Workplace Learning, Community Education, and Research.

LOCAL ADULT LEARNING BOARDS

Thirty-three Local Adult Education Boards will be established throughout the country to promote a co-ordinated area-based approach to the delivery of adult education services, to promote and develop comprehensive information services, to ensure complementarity with training and employment services and to provide organisational, administrative, professional and financial support to adult education services in the area. The Boards will report annually to the National Adult Learning Council on the delivery of services in their regions

Membership of the Local Boards will include representation from social partners, education and training providers, learners, community and voluntary pillar interests, Traveller and disability organisations, area partnerships, library services, health boards and adult literacy interests.

The Local Adult Learning Boards will be established as statutory sub-committees of the VECs. They will function as autonomous sub-committees which are administratively hosted by the VEC, and where the VEC also provides a technical service as the employer of additional staff appointed to the Boards. The Boards will have authority to make decisions on the deployment of resources within each region in regard to designated programmes within the Further Education sector. In addition, Local Adult Learning Boards will be required to ensure parity of esteem between the different interest groups, and that each member of the Board has full and equal status.

The Local Adult Learning Boards will be required to formally convene local **community fora** through which the views of a wide range of interests can be channelled. The fora should be convened by way of public meetings to which all interest groups with a role in adult education should be invited.

In view of the expansion of activity, the extra work associated with the role of the Local Adult Learning Boards and the need to promote an enhanced adult learning dimension to the role of community, comprehensive and secondary schools, a further **thirty-five Adult Education Officers** will be appointed. Of these 33 will be appointed to the Local Adult Learning Boards on a flexible needs basis, to be deployed in accordance with the priorities for the region identified by the Boards locally. The local Adult Education Officers will pay particular attention to the need to convene local networks of secondary, and community and comprehensive schools and develop good linkages with the other stakeholders and providers in the area, supporting and promoting an increased role for these sectors in the provision of adult learning. This work will be further supported through the appointment of the remaining two adult education officers to the National Adult Learning Council to co-ordinate this task at a national level and ensure a democratic and streamlined framework for representation of these sectors in the work of the Local Adult Learning Boards and that of the National Council. Provision of appropriate staff development programmes, networking in national fora, and co-ordination of policy inputs and responses will be part of this task, working in close collaboration with the Department, the NALC and the relevant management bodies.

The Local Adult Learning Boards will have a key role to play in ensuring a co-ordinated area-based input in respect of adult education into the strategic plans to be developed by the County/City Development Boards.

Given the expansion of services in this area in recent times, and the new developments now proposed, a comprehensive assessment will be undertaken in relation to professional and administrative staffing levels in VECs.

PRIORITIES

Adult Education is the last area of mass education which remains to be developed in Ireland, and it will require significantly increased investment on a phased basis if adult learning opportunities are to reach a stage of parity with those in other countries. In facing such a challenge the top priorities are:-

- to allocate priority resources to addressing adult literacy needs;

- to systematically increase opportunities for adult learners within the system, prioritising the needs of those with less than upper secondary education;

- to develop supporting services such as adult guidance and counselling and childcare;

- to enhance the responsiveness, relevance and flexibility of education and training provision to meet the needs of young people and adults alike, optimising participation of and benefit to, those at risk;

- to promote and develop a co-ordinated integrated role for adult education and training as a vital component within an over-arching framework for lifelong learning.

The programme of change and development set out in this White Paper will be implemented on a phased basis in the light of the resources made available in the context of the National Development Plan and the annual Estimates for Public Services provisions.

Introduction

Adult Education in an Era of Lifelong Learning (1998) was the first Green Paper on Adult Education since the foundation of the State. It was followed by an extensive consultation process to obtain the views of a diverse range of interests on its contents and on the principles and strategies which should underpin the future development of Adult Education in Ireland. The Government is now pleased to publish the country's first White Paper on Adult Education.

The publication of this White Paper marks the adoption of lifelong learning as the governing principle of educational policy. Coming just a year and a half after the Green Paper, it is further evidence of the Government's commitment to placing Adult Education firmly on the country's educational agenda. It follows the recent publication of a *White Paper on Early Childhood Education: Ready to Learn, 1999* and will make an important contribution to informing and enabling the Government to put in place, for the first time, systematic and comprehensive provision for lifelong learning. Together the two White Papers draw attention to the official recognition by the State that its educational commitment now extends to include not only those in school, college or training, but also that part of the population which has yet to go to school and that which has left the initial education system. This is truly a new departure by the State in shaping its educational thinking and policies. It indicates a shift from a solely front-loading model of educational provision to one in which lifelong learning becomes the overriding principle.

The Adult Education sector has shown itself to be highly creative, talented and relevant to meeting the educational objectives of diverse groups of society. It has pioneered curricula, methodologies and alliances which not only merit recognition in themselves but which pose challenges and provide models of best practice, to the other education sectors. The success of the sector as an expression of the combined expertise and resource of a multiplicity of providers, statutory and non-statutory, is also noted as a cornerstone not only to its achievements to date, but, also, to its future health and well being.

This White Paper commits the Government to a multi-faceted sectoral development programme in Adult Education with immediate effect. In meeting the demands from society, particularly in areas concerning citizenship, social inclusion and skill needs, the task now lies in securing the successes of the sector; in retaining its user-driven

Chapter 1
Adult Education

CHAPTER 1
Adult Education

1.1 This is Ireland's first White Paper on Adult Education. It is testimony to a recognition by the Government of the fact that:-

- the Adult Education sector has a major contribution to make to meeting the skill requirements of a rapidly changing workforce, and to the dominant national concerns of social cohesion and equity in the emergence of a broadly inclusive and pro-active civil society;

- the sector has shown itself to be highly creative, effective, challenging and relevant;

- concerns to promote a framework for lifelong learning, and critically to cater for the needs of adults within it, are increasingly moving centre stage in countries throughout the developed world.

This Chapter will:-

- specify the aims of the White Paper;

- propose a definition of Adult Education;

- explore the significance of the role of Adult Education in contributing to the overall vision of modern Irish society;

- elaborate on the key principles upon which the White Paper is based;

- provide an overview of the educational attainment of the Irish adult population.

1.2 AIMS

This White Paper aims to provide a template for the development of the Adult Education sector as part of an overall Government commitment to establishing a comprehensive system of lifelong learning for all. Specifically, the Paper will:-

- reflect on the role of Adult Education in the context of an overall vision for the development of this society;

- build on the consultation process surrounding the *Green Paper on Adult Education: Adult Education in an Era of Lifelong Learning 1998* (hereafter referred to as the Green Paper), focusing in particular on the needs of the learners;

- set out the Government priorities and the framework for the future development of the sector, based on the feedback from the consultation process;

- identify the priority areas for public investment in Adult Education, in the light of a rapidly changing societal and cultural context and in the context of an overall commitment to lifelong learning;

- identify priority groups and programme areas and set targets for implementation;

- elaborate upon the roles of various providers in the field and the supports they require;

- provide for a learner-centred framework incorporating infrastructural elements such as guidance and counselling, quality assurance and the training of trainers, and ensuring a coherent range of pathways for adults between education and training and other relevant supports;

- propose a comprehensive structural framework at national and local level for the support and development of Adult Education;

- set adult education in the context of an overall continuum of quality education services from early childhood through to and throughout, adulthood, as an integral element of a framework for lifelong learning.

While this Paper bridges the traditional divide between education and training, it does not aim to provide a policy blueprint for the training aspects of the field, given that this task is being advanced through the *National Employment Action Plans (1998, 1999, 2000)*, and previous publications, and through the work of the Task Force on Lifelong Learning. The Paper seeks, however, to ensure that there is a fit and complementarity between education and training provision so as to enable the learner to move progressively and incrementally within an overarching, co-ordinated and learner-centred framework.

1.3 DEFINITION

For the purposes of this Paper, Adult Education is defined as *"systematic learning undertaken by adults who return to learning having concluded initial education or training"*. The concept is intended to encapsulate:-

- **re-entry by adults to Further Education**: i.e. education and training which occurs between second and third-level. This includes programmes such as Post Leaving Certificate courses, second-chance education such as the

Vocational Training Opportunities Scheme for the unemployed, Adult Literacy and Basic Education, and self-funded adult education programmes;

re-entry by adults to Higher Education;

Continuing Education and Training: i.e. professional or vocational development of people in the workforce or re-entering the workforce; regardless of the level;

Community Education: i.e. the process whereby marginalised groups formulate a process of user-driven, learner-centred and communal education;

other systematic and deliberate learning undertaken by adults in a wide variety of settings and contexts, both formal and informal.

The underpinning theme in this definition is centred on the adult learner's *re-engagement* having exited from the system at an earlier stage in life.

1.4 ADULT EDUCATION WITHIN AN OVERALL VISION FOR THE SOCIETY

1.4.1 This White Paper advocates a national programme of Adult Education within an overall framework of lifelong learning on the basis of its contribution to six priority areas of:-

Consciousness Raising;

Citizenship;

Cohesion;

Competitiveness;

Cultural Development;

Community Building.

1.4.2 Consciousness Raising

Consciousness raising refers to the capacity of Adult Education to enable people to realise their full human potential in a way that draws on the links between their individual personal experiences and wider structural factors. It embraces a view of

Adult Education as an empowering process of self-discovery towards personal and collective development.

1.4.3 Citizenship

Citizenship refers to the role of Adult Education in enabling individual members of the society to grow in self-confidence, social awareness and social responsibility and to take an active role in shaping the overall direction of the society - culturally, socially and economically and environmentally - and to engage proactively in community and societal decision-making.

1.4.4 Cohesion

Cohesion focuses on enhancing social capital in general, but particularly on the empowerment of those experiencing significant disadvantage, in order that they may play a full and active part in all areas of the social and economic life of the country. This is both an educational and an organisational challenge.

1.4.5 Competitiveness

Competitiveness concerns the role of Adult Education in providing a skilled workforce to meet the needs of a knowledge society, and in promoting prosperity, employment and growth. Investment in education and training plays a critical role in supporting society's capacity for adaptability and change. The skill levels and quality of the workforce are increasingly viewed as providing the cutting edge in competing in the global economy. All industrialised countries now recognise the continuous upskilling of the workforce as a priority. Equally, they are increasingly moving from a traditional skills focus in their ongoing training policies for workers, recognising the validity of a broadly-based, investigative learning model focused not only on specific task related skills but on personal development and interpersonal issues.

1.4.6 Cultural Development

Cultural development refers to the role of Adult Education in enriching the cultural fabric of society; in developing an appreciation and an understanding of cultural and artistic forms and artistic literacy within the population and in defining national identity within an open, pluralist and globalising context.

1.4.7 Community Development

Community development refers to the contribution of Adult Education to the development of a structural analysis and a collective sense of purpose amongst marginalised people who share common problems and who aim to become actively involved in solving these problems.

1.5 CORE PRINCIPLES

1.5.1 This White Paper is underpinned by three core principles concerning Adult Education, namely:-

(a) Lifelong Learning as a Systemic Approach

(b) Equality

(c) Inter-culturalism

1.5.2 Systemic Approach

This White Paper marks the adoption for the first time of a commitment to lifelong learning as the governing principle of Irish education policy, and as having a pivotal position in the overall Irish economic and social strategy. The significance of the White Paper, then, extends beyond the sectoral concerns of Adult Education only, to include a concern with the early school experience also. The *White Paper on Early Childhood Education Ready to Learn (1999)* locates its commitment to early childhood education within an overall concern for the development of a continuum of lifelong learning.

A commitment to a lifelong learning agenda as a relatively seamless progression through an educational continuum from the cradle to the grave, with open boundaries between the worlds of home/work/education and provision for flexibility in learning sources, raises challenges not only for tertiary education but also for early life education. The early school experience provides the fundamental foundation for educational progress in later years. Failure at this stage, in terms of acquiring a positive disposition to learning; in acquiring the fundamental learning tools of literacy and numeracy; in developing a positive sense of personal well-being and the requisite interpersonal and social skills needed to participate in the everyday life of the community, can very seriously limit the life chances of children. While adult and general out-of-school education interventions have shown that such negative early school experiences can be redressed, it is clearly far better that these needs are met in the early school life of the person, with the emphasis on prevention.

Successful education in school shares many of the qualities which are characteristic of the best forms of Adult Education. These would include the following:-

- an holistic curriculum, focused on a broad sphere of learning and on catering for the learner's educational and personal needs in a way which reflects his/her cultural and community context and experience;

- a view of the student as a self-directed, self-motivated learner;

White Paper on Adult Education – Learning for Life

- a recognition of the student as the centre of the learning process, being supported by teachers and other learners rather than as one in pursuit of the learning which others have already acquired - i.e. learning as *construction* rather than as *instruction*. Participative models for identifying and adapting provision to learner needs are central to this process;

- a core learning objective of preparing the learner for a life of learning rather than for a terminal, end-of-learning examination;

- new models of assessment and greater fluidity between the educational sectors themselves and between these and the other domains particularly of work and home;

- the development of the community dimension of provision, with integrated linkages between the work of the education centre/school and those of youth, adult and community interests, and with other agencies in the community, particularly in the employment, health and welfare and local development fields;

- a key focus on support for learners at major transition points - from primary to second-level, from school to work or further education/training, from unemployment to employment;

- the promotion of high standards of achievement for all students, irrespective of background.

Within a lifelong learning framework of reference all forms of formal education need to pay more overt attention to such features of the educational process. This relates to pupils' encounter with learning during the vitally formative years of schooling itself, but also, so that they are equipped to continue as more self-reliant learners throughout their lives.

A lifelong learning agenda redefines the school as one of many agencies and learning sites involved with the learner in a much more fluid and less time specific way than has been the case traditionally.

The Green Paper characterised lifelong learning as a process incorporating three dimensions, namely:-

Lifelong

Lifewide

Voluntary and self-motivated

Lifelong

The lifelong dimension of Adult and Community Education refers to its place within a continuum of education from the cradle to the grave. It highlights the need to formulate education strategies which encompass the person's life-cycle, and challenges educational systems to be adaptive to the changing life-cycle requirements of learners and to ensuring that students in their early school experience acquire both the disposition and the capacity for lifelong learning.

Lifewide

The lifewide dimension of lifelong learning refers to the multiplicity of sites in which learning now occurs. With regard to adult learning it encompasses the school or other conventional educational institutions, training centres, the home (particularly through I.T. or other forms of home-based learning), the community and the workplace.

Lifewide education poses particular systemic challenges. These include the appropriate resourcing of different learning sites, recognising that while learning can occur spontaneously in any variety of settings, economies of scale and quality assurance issues will always require some selection and designation of providers. It also requires ease of movement and progression between learning sites based on parity of esteem between providers; the development of methods of assessment of learning independently of the context in which such learning occurs; the need to provide the requisite infra-structural supports to the learner in the form of guidance and counselling; the provision of childcare and transport and appropriate mechanisms of accreditation and assessment.

Voluntary and self-motivated

Adult learning is primarily undertaken on a voluntary self-motivated basis and in a context where the learner rather than the provider is at the centre of the process. This White Paper aims to secure the learner-centred aspect of Adult Education in the approaches and the policies it proposes. Such a user-driven commitment challenges the predominance of institutional providers in determining the context and methodologies of the learning experience; it transforms the power relationships between the provider and the learner in favour of the learner and it challenges institutions to develop and implement inclusive policies and practice and processes of learner engagement.

It is clear, then, that an approach to Adult Education within a lifelong learning framework raises profound and fundamental challenges not only in the design of an appropriate system for Adult Education but also for its interrelationships and systemic linkages with other sectors of the education and training system. In an organisational sense it requires that blockages to educational progression be removed. People who find themselves in educational cul-de-sacs due to:-

- previous achievements within the formal education system;

- current domestic or workplace commitments, or

- age or other life cycle considerations

are the main concerns in developing a policy for Adult Education. While the Irish education system has many recognised strengths, there are inherent inflexibilities within it, in terms of the predominance of full-time options, low participation of mature students in third-level, and difficulties with access and progression for those who hold qualifications other than the Leaving Certificate. While there have been many recent welcome initiatives in the second-level curriculum and in the emergence of a range of accredited out-of-school programmes, such as Youthreach and VTOS, it is essential to continue to enhance progression opportunities for students who have left the initial system having failed in it or been failed by it.

1.5.3 Equality

The Government recognises that barriers arising from differences of socio-economic status, ethnicity, disability and gender continue to hinder the emergence of a fully inclusive and cohesive society. Considering the significance of educational attainment in a society where qualifications are becoming ever more important, inequalities in educational opportunities and attainment arising from such barriers are a major concern.

Inequalities in education due to socio-economic differences have been well documented and this Chapter presents an overview of current educational attainment levels of Irish adults. Clearly, if Adult Education is to counteract the impact of disadvantage in early school participation and achievement, there must be careful targeting of initiatives on those most in need. Such targeting is a central pillar of the National Anti-Poverty Strategy, and is reflected also in the key principles underpinning the £194m package of measures to address educational disadvantage published by Government in December 1999. These measures address every level of education from early childhood to adult literacy and third- level education.

1.5.4 Inter-culturalism

Ireland has undergone profound social, cultural and economic changes in recent decades as it transforms itself into an open and rapidly modernising society. While this change has proven to be challenging and sometimes traumatic, involving the transformation of many traditional certitudes and frames of reference it has been accompanied, particularly in recent years, by a heightened sense of national self-esteem and by a growing conviction of the innate value of Irish cultural and art forms.

The growing openness of Irish society, coupled with the growing phenomenon of

Wicklow County Council
County Library Services

immigration particularly from non-traditional sources poses new challenges to the nature of the Irish identity, introducing a dimension of ethnic and racial diversity heretofore unknown in the country. As observed in the Delors Commission, the realisation that *"my neighbour may no longer be like me"* may come as a shock.

The challenge of an inter-cultural education is to simultaneously acknowledge and celebrate the cultural heritage unique to each different ethnic group while contributing to a shared collective awareness of nationhood. It must work towards a view of difference as something to be celebrated and which is enriching to the totality of the society rather than as the basis for enmity.

1.6 EDUCATIONAL STATUS OF THE IRISH ADULT POPULATION

1.6.1 Adult Literacy

The *OECD International Adult Literacy Survey (IALS, 1997)* focused public attention and urgency on the adult literacy problem in Ireland. On a scale of 1-5 the survey, which was carried out in Ireland in 1995, found that about 25% of the Irish population scored at the lowest level (Level 1) in the document scale with a further 32% at Level 2. (The IALS document scale tested the knowledge and skills required to locate and use information contained in various formats such as official forms, timetables, maps and charts.) The percentage at Level 1 was the highest for any country studied except for Poland. The survey also drew attention to:-

- the substantially lower levels of literacy in older age groups;

- the close links between lower scores and lower educational levels;

- an association between low income and low literacy levels;

- an association between low levels of literacy and low levels of participation in second-chance education and training.

1.6.2 Upper Second-Level

The expansion in post-compulsory education in Ireland in recent years has been dramatic. In 1966, 55% of the population had finished their education at under the age of 15, whereas, currently, over 81% of school-leavers annually have completed Leaving Certificate. The consequence of this change is a widening gap in educational attainment between younger and older age groups.

Table 1:1

PERCENTAGE OF THE POPULATION COMPLETING AT LEAST UPPER SECONDARY EDUCATION BY AGE GROUP (1998)

	25-64	25-34	35-44	45-54	55-64
Australia	56	64	58	52	44
Austria	73	84	78	68	56
Belgium	57	73	61	51	34
Canada	80	87	83	77	65
Czech Republic	85	92	88	84	74
Denmark	78	85	80	78	67
Finland	68	84	78	62	41
France	61	75	63	56	41
Germany	84	88	87	84	76
Greece	44	66	52	36	22
Hungary	63	77	73	65	31
Iceland	55	61	58	55	40
Ireland	51	67	56	41	31
Italy	41	55	50	35	19
Japan	80	93	91	77	57
Korea	65	92	70	45	27
Mexico	21	26	23	16	9
Netherlands	64	74	68	59	50
New Zealand	73	79	77	69	58
Norway	83	93	88	78	65
Poland	54	62	59	53	37
Portugal	20	29	20	14	12
Spain	33	53	38	23	12
Sweden	76	87	80	73	60
Switzerland	81	88	83	80	71
Turkey	18	24	19	13	7
United Kingdom	60	63	62	58	53
United States	86	88	88	87	80
Country Mean	**61**	**72**	**65**	**57**	**44**

Source: OECD (2000) Education at a Glance: OECD Indicators 2000 . Paris

As the above table shows, 31% of those currently aged between 55 and 64 have completed second-level education in Ireland as opposed to 67% of the 25-34 age cohort. This pattern is common throughout many OECD countries, reflecting the very significantly increased investment and participation in second-level education since the 1960s throughout the industrialised world. These figures draw attention to one of the most pervasive and persistent inequalities throughout the industrialised world - that of aged-based differentials in educational attainment. Apart from considerations of social justice raised by such differences in attainment, the task of upgrading the educational attainment levels of those aged between 25 and 64 also has significant economic implications, particularly with regard to the reduced relative competitiveness of countries which fail to do so. The table shows that while there has been a dramatic increase in participation rates in completion of upper second-level education in the 25-34 year age group relative to the 55-64 age group, Ireland's relative ranking within the OECD countries shown remains relatively unchanged, i.e. the improvements were matched by similar or larger increases in participation overseas. Ireland is ranked 22nd of OECD countries in terms of the population aged 25-64 who have completed upper secondary education, 18th in terms of the 25-34 age group, and 22nd for the 35-44 age group.

The OECD projects the proportion of adults in the 25-64 age group who would have completed secondary education in the year 2015 based on 1995 graduation rates. Notwithstanding some definitional ambiguity regarding what constitutes upper second-level, Ireland ranks 15th of the 20 countries studied based on 1995 completion rates, with only Portugal, Spain, Australia, Italy and Greece in less favourable positions.

Table 1:2

PROJECTED GROWTH IN THE EDUCATIONAL LEVELS OF THE ADULT POPULATION

Percentage of the population aged 25-64 having completed upper secondary education (assuming 1995 youth qualification rates)

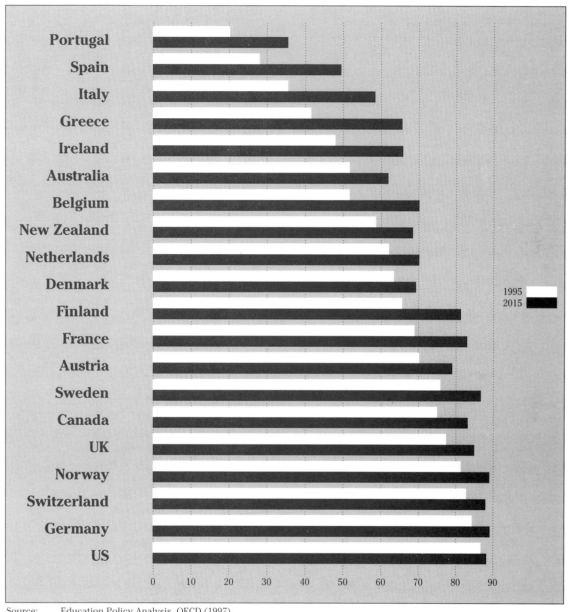

Source: Education Policy Analysis. OECD (1997)

The above table shows how the task of upgrading educational attainment levels is a slow process if one concentrates solely on increasing participation among today's youth cohorts. Upgrading attainment levels more quickly also requires expanding Adult Education opportunities.

1.6.3 Third-level Education

In relation to those with a third-level education, the position is as follows:-

Table 1:3

DISTRIBUTION OF THE POPULATION 25 TO 64 YEARS OF AGE WHO HAVE COMPLETED THIRD-LEVEL EDUCATION (1998)

	At least Certificate/Diploma-level Education	At least Degree-level Education
Australia	25	17
Austria (2)	11	6
Belgium	25	12
Canada	39	19
Czech Republic	10	10
Denmark	25	5
Finland (2)	29	13
France	21	11
Germany	23	14
Greece (2)	16	11
Hungary	13	13
Iceland	21	16
Ireland (2)	**21**	**11**
Italy (3)	9	9
Japan	30	18
Korea	22	17
Mexico	13	12
Netherlands (3)	24	24
New Zealand	27	13
Norway (2)	26	24
Poland (3)	11	11
Portugal	9	7
Spain	20	14
Sweden	28	13
Switzerland	23	14
Turkey (3)	6	6
United Kingdom	24	15
United States	35	27
Country mean	**21**	**14**

Source: OECD (2000), Education at a Glance: OECD Indicators 2000, Paris

1. The category "at least degree level" includes degree level and advanced research programmes.
2. Year of reference 1997
3. The level of educational attainment of degree level includes Certificate/Diploma level.

White Paper on Adult Education – Learning for Life

Ireland is ranked 16th within the OECD countries in terms of the proportion of population aged 25-64 with third-level education, but for the 25-34 age group the ranking is 11th.

1.6.4 Quarterly National Household Survey March-May 1999

Table 1:4 below shows the highest educational levels of the population in the 15-64 age group: -

Table 1:4 – HIGHEST EDUCATIONAL LEVELS OF POPULATION 15-64

	At Work	Unemployed	Not in Labour Force	Total
Below lower secondary	210,100 13.5%	30,400 31.4%	289,200 34.4%	529,600 21.2%
Lower secondary	313,300 20.1%	29,100 30.1%	247,200 29.4%	589,500 23.6%
Upper Secondary completed	446,800 28.7%	20,100 20.8%	193.900 23.1%	660,800 26.5%
Further Ed/training	189,700 12.2%	8,000 8.3%	42,400 5.1%	240,100 9.6%
Third-level non-degree	129,800 8.3%	4,000 4.1%	26,600 2.8%	157,300 6.3%
Degree or above	234,800 15.1%	3,800 3.9%	29,900 3.6%	268,400 10.8%
Other/ not stated	33,000 2.1%	1,400 1.4%	13,600 1.6%	48,000 1.9%
Total	1,557,500 100%	96,700 100%	839,600 100%	2,493,800 100%

Source: CSO Quarterly National Household Survey Q2 1999

Appendix 1 shows this information by sex and by age bands. It will be seen that for women not in the labour force, 27.7% (157,400) are in the age bands 25-54 and have less than upper secondary education. The corresponding figure for men in the same age band is 16.1%. For both sexes, the risk of not being in the labour force or being unemployed reduces sharply as qualification levels increase.

1.6.5 Early School Leaving

For a variety of reasons, Irish adults, as shown in the Green Paper, compare unfavourably with those of most industrialised countries in terms of their formal education levels. Equally, there continues to be unacceptably high levels of underachievement and dropout from second-level schools. Of the almost 70,000 school leavers who left school in 1996/97, 13,300 (19%) left without a Leaving Certificate. Of these, 2,500 (3.5%) left with no second-level qualification. In addition, an estimated 800 failed to transfer from primary to second-level school. Early school leavers encounter greater difficulties in accessing further education and training opportunities and are far more vulnerable to unemployment - those with no qualifications are six times more likely to be unemployed than labour market entrants with a Leaving Certificate. While the Government is committed to maximising second-level completion for those up to 18 years old, it is also concerned that those who have not completed second-level should have the opportunity to progress their education or training through a parallel or alternative route up to and including higher education. The concept of a terminal qualification is incompatible with a commitment to lifelong learning.

1.6.6 Socio-economic Differences

Inequalities in education due to socio-economic differences have been well documented in the literature. For instance, Clancy, citing the report of the *Technical Working Group on Higher Education (1995)* draws attention to the wide socio-economic differences in educational attainment in the second-level sector. As the following table shows, children from unskilled and skilled manual backgrounds are less likely than all other groups to reach Leaving Certificate level and, having reached this level, significantly less likely to achieve 2Cs at honours level.

White Paper on Adult Education – Learning for Life

Table 1:5

EDUCATIONAL TRANSITIONS: DIFFERENTIAL PARTICIPATION AND ACHIEVEMENT RATES BY FATHER'S SOCIO-ECONOMIC GROUP

Father's Socio-Economic Group	% Reaching Leaving Cert Level	Of those Reaching Leaving Cert Level.		Of those with at least 5 passes in Leaving Cert. % enrolled in Higher Education	Of those with at least 2Cs at Hon. Level % enrolled in Higher Education
		% with at least 5 Passes	Of those with at least 5 passes in Leaving Cert. % enrolled in Higher Education		
Farmers	88.3	91.3	56.8	48.5	66.6
Other Agricultural	63.0	90.2	38.0	33.7	71.4
Higher Professional	97.1	92.8	80.1	76.8	84.1
Lower Professional	95.7	95.5	74.9	61.0	73.7
Employers and Managers	90.7	90.3	65.1	62.2	76.1
Salaried Employees	93.2	93.3	61.8	53.0	70.9
Intermediate Non-Manual	84.3	91.7	60.8	51.1	70.4
Other Non-Manual	70.5	87.7	42.2	32.4	57.6
Skilled Manual	75.9	89.2	41.4	35.9	63.3
Semi –Skilled Manual	61.7	80	28	30	57.1
Unskilled Manual	52.5	79.1	28.8	23.0	55.8
TOTAL*	78.0	89.5	52.6	46.3	69.5

Source: Clancy (1995) Interim Report of the Steering Committee's Technical Working Group. HEA

The Green Paper also drew attention both to the socio-economic nature of educational underachievement and to its intergenerational character. Drawing on the *OECD Economic Survey of Ireland (1995)* it showed that:-

47% of children from unskilled manual backgrounds left
School with Junior Certificate or less as opposed to 29%
from higher professional backgrounds;

8% of children from "low status" backgrounds
achieved 5 honours or more in the Leaving Certificate,
compared with 26.3% from "higher status" background.

The ESRI Annual School Leaver Surveys also consistently show that it is the children of the unemployed who are most at risk themselves of becoming unemployed, while the children of fathers in the higher socio-economic groups are most likely to progress to third-level education. In addition, both the level of education attained and the grades achieved at Junior and Leaving Certificate level influence the length of time spent seeking work, the duration of periods of unemployment, and levels of earnings.

There is substantial evidence from the OECD *(Education at a Glance 2000)* that those who got the most formal education are also more likely to receive training as adults: three times as many employees with a tertiary qualification participate in continuing education and training as employees with less than an upper secondary qualification. On average, over 4 times as many people at Literacy Levels 4 and 5 in the International Adult Literacy Surveys participated in adult education and training education compared with those on the lowest literacy level (document scale).

This situation leads the OECD to the conclusion that current patterns of participation in continuing education and training are likely to exacerbate rather than reduce learning inequalities.

1.6.7 Gender differences

The *ESRI 1998 Annual School Leavers Survey* shows that 64% of those who leave school early with no qualifications are boys, and this pattern is mirrored for those who leave with a Junior Certificate but before completion of the Leaving Certificate. In terms of examination results, girls consistently outperform boys in the aggregate grades achieved in the Junior Certificate and Leaving Certificate examinations. Traditional patterns of subject choice are still evident, with girls being under-represented in Applied Mathematics, Chemistry, Agricultural Science, Economics and subjects in the construction field, and boys under-represented in Home Economics and Biology, Art and Languages. The *1998 Annual School Leavers Survey* shows that 44.9% of all female leavers progressed to further study compared with 33.7% of boys. 55.2% of male leavers entered employment, compared with 38.9% of girls. When those not entering the labour market are discounted, higher employment levels are still recorded for boys, notwithstanding their general lower educational attainment levels. In addition, a general pattern of higher average weekly earnings levels for boys emerges.

OECD data show that in Ireland women are outnumbered by men at Certificate/Diploma and Ph.D award levels, but women slightly outnumber men at first degree and Masters award levels.

Table 1:6

PERCENTAGES OF NON-DEGREE AND DEGREE-LEVEL QUALIFICATIONS IN EACH SUBJECT CATEGORY THAT ARE AWARDED TO WOMEN (1998)

	Health and Welfare		Life sciences, physical sciences and agriculture		Maths and computer science		Humanities arts and education		Social sciences, business, law and services		Engineering, manu-facturing and construction		All areas of study		
	Cert Dip	Deg	Cert Dip	Deg	Cert Dip	Deg	Cert Dip	Deg	Cert Dip	Deg	Cert Dip	Deg	Cert Dip	1st Deg	Ph.D
Ireland	85	68	54	54	55	37	70	65	56	54	10	21	48	54	41
Country Mean	84	65	38	45	30	31	72	69	58	49	15	21	59	53	34

Source: OECD (2000) Education at a Glance, 2000.

Moreover, as the above table shows, there is a number of discipline areas where females significantly outnumber men – Health and Welfare, the Humanities, Arts and Education. Women, however, continue to be poorly represented in Engineering, Manufacturing and Construction and in the Mathematics and Computer Science fields at degree level.

While more women than men across all age groups have at least upper second-level education, (albeit below the OECD mean) the table below shows the pattern is reversed at third-level, with some improvement in participation of women being evident in the younger age groups.

Table 1:7

EDUCATIONAL ATTAINMENT BY SEX AND AGE GROUP (1998)

AT LEAST UPPER SECOND-LEVEL	Age 25-34	35-44	45-54	55-64	25-64
Ireland					
Men	63	52	39	30	48
Women	71	60	42	32	54
Country Mean					
Men	72	67	61	50	64
Women	72	63	52	38	58
AT LEAST DEGREE LEVEL					
Ireland					
Men	17	13	9	6	12
Women	15	9	6	4	9
Country Mean					
Men	16	17	16	12	15
Women	16	13	10	6	12

Source: OECD (2000) Education at a Glance 2000.

Within the third-level sector, a recent study undertaken on behalf of the Commission on the Points System on the correlation between performance in the Leaving Certificate and performance in higher education, shows that gender and field of study both have an influence on performance. Whereas 62% of those studying Humanities obtained at least a second class honours/merit result, the equivalent proportion for other faculties combined was just 28%. While there were no significant differences by gender in terms of completion rates, males achieved proportionally more high final grades than females – 39% of males obtained at least a higher second class honour/merit compared to 29% of females. The gender differential was stronger in the university sector and varied by field of study.

Overall, the Employment Equality Agency Report *Women in the Labour Force 1999* shows that women earn 75% of men's earnings in the industrial sector, and that only 3% hold the position of managing director.

With regard to adult women's participation in education and training, as Table 1:8 shows, women in Ireland generally are more likely than men to participate in continuing education and training whether they are employed or unemployed. Unemployed women aged 25-64 are nearly three times more likely to participate in education and training than similarly aged unemployed men.

Table 1:8

PERCENTAGE OF 25 TO 64 YEAR OLDS PARTICIPATING IN EDUCATION AND TRAINING IN THE PREVIOUS YEAR BY CURRENT PRIMARY WORK SITUATION, GENDER AND AGE (1994-1995)

All Education and Training

	25-64 year olds			25-44 year olds		
	Employed	Unemployed	All	Employed	Unemployed	All
Ireland						
M-W	30	9	22	31	11	27
Men	25	6	20	27	9	24
Women	37	17	24	38	20	30

Source: OECD (1998) Education at a Glance, 1998

It should be noted, however, that there are substantial numbers of women not in the labour force. Women in the home continue to face significant barriers in areas such as childcare, care of other dependants, finance and transport in accessing education and training opportunities. Women with low levels of education tend to experience the greatest inequalities in labour market participation. Men with low levels of education are far more likely to be in the labour force than women with the same levels of education. Apart from the immediate impact of such barriers on women's life chances, there is substantial evidence also concerning the influence of the mother's education on the educational development of the child.

With regard to female participation in State-funded Adult Education, training and employment programmes, as the following table shows, females are still in the minority in these programmes, accounting for 44% of participants. Generally, they are under-represented on the training and employment schemes, accounting for 39% overall in these categories, but accounting for 66% of participation in educational provision. Female participation is relatively high on most FÁS programmes, with the exception of Apprenticeship (notwithstanding the availability of bursaries) and targeted employment schemes which are confined to very specific eligibility categories. The FÁS Positive Action Programme has significantly increased female participation in mainstream training in recent years.

However, in general terms, the use of Live Register status criteria to govern access to a range of labour market education and training programmes, allied with the absence of childcare provision, continue to pose significant barriers for women. The *OECD International Adult Literacy Survey: Results for Ireland 1997* shows that in Ireland, 33.7% of males participating in Adult Education or training were self-financed, but the comparable figure for females was 49%.

The *National Development Plan 2000-2006* sets out a range of measures to promote equality of opportunity in education and training and to address barriers in regard to childcare. These are referred to later in this Paper in Sections 2.11.3 and 8.9.

TABLE 1:9

OVERALL FEMALE PARTICIPATION RATES IN MAIN EDUCATION, TRAINING AND EMPLOYMENT PROGRAMMES

COURSE/PROGRAMME/ TRAINING TITLE	PROVIDER	STATS RELATE TO:	TOTAL	MALE	FEMALE	% FEMALE (Rounded)
EDUCATIONAL PROVISION						
Back to Education Allowance -Second-level Option	DSCFA	At Feb. 99	476	191	285	60%
Back to Education Allowance -Third-level Option	DSCFA	At Feb. 99	4107	2259	1758	44%
Vocational Training Opportunities Scheme	Dept.Ed. & Sc.	At Jan 99	4580	1873	2707	59%
Post Leaving Cert Courses	Dept.Ed. & Sc.	98/99	23810	6960	16850	71%
		Subtotal	**32883**	**11283**	**21600**	**66%**
TRAINING PROVISION						
Specific Skills Training	FÁS	Throughput 1998	11537	6659	4878	42%
Traineeship	FÁS	Throughput 1998	1265	682	593	46%
Standards Based Apprenticeship	FÁS	Throughput 1998	7147	7097	50	0.7%
Community Training Workshop	FÁS	Throughput 1998	2125	1157	968	46%
Community Training Programme	FÁS	Throughput 1998	4002	2104	1898	47%
Return to Work Scheme	FÁS	Throughput 1998	1113	48	1065	96%
Enterprise Training	FÁS	Throughput 1998	592	188	404	68%
Job Training Programme	FÁS	Throughput 1998	1213	566	647	53%
Elementary Training for Tourism/Catering Industry	CERT	Throughput 1998	1276	568	708	55%
Rural Tourism & Food Enterprise Programmes	TEAGASC	Throughput 1998	1281	477	804	63%
Agricultural – Short Course Provision	TEAGASC	Throughput 1998	1365	552	813	60%
		Subtotal	**33591**	**20354**	**13237**	**39%**
EMPLOYMENT SCHEMES						
Community Employment - Part Time Integration Option	FÁS	1998 Throughput	36044	14979	21065	58%
Community Employment - Part Time Job Option	FÁS	1998 Throughput	15795	10416	5379	34%
Job Initiative	FÁS	1998 Throughput	1154	719	435	38%
Jobstart	FÁS	1998 Throughput	1469	903	566	38%
Workplace	FÁS	1998 Throughput	1452	806	646	44%
Family Income Supplement	DSCFA	At April 99	13829	7947	5882	43%
Part Time Job Incentive Scheme	DSCFA	At Feb 99	563	N/A	N/A	N/A
Back to Work Allowance/ Back to Work Enterprise Allowance	DSCFA	At April 99	26833	23006	3827	14%
		Subtotal	**97139**	**58776**	**37800**	**39%**
TOTALS		**OVERALL TOTALS**	**163613**	**90413**	**72637**	**44%**

Source: Report of the P2000 Working Group on Women's Access to Labour Market Opportunities, 2000

1.6.8 Participation of People with Disabilities, Travellers and other Minority Groups

The equality proofing of Adult Education provision begins with a commitment to the rights of minorities. People with disabilities, Travellers and other minority groups continue to experience serious problems in education generally and in Adult Education in particular. An equality proofing commitment would address access and outcomes for such groups as an entitlement rather than a concession: would assemble all statistical data with a focus on the participation of minorities and would link funding to providers on the basis of their capacity to meet equality criteria and to realise defined targets in the participation of minorities.

People with disabilities are to be found in all sectors of the population. Historically their segregation in training, education and employment has excluded them from mainstream provision. By focusing exclusively on their disability this approach has also served to obscure their particular needs as members of other disadvantaged groups. Ensuring equal access for people with disabilities in Adult Education requires an integrated response across the full range of provision. In order to access Adult Education as an entitlement, adults with disabilities may need additional and appropriate supports to overcome difficulties that relate specifically to the nature of their disability. The provision of such supports should be taken into account in assessing commitment to equality on the part of providers.

The Employment Equality Act 1998 outlaws discrimination on nine distinct grounds — gender, marital status, family status, disability, sexual orientation, age, religion, race, and membership of the Traveller community. The Equal Status Act, 2000 addresses issues of inequality and discrimination in the provision of goods and services. The Equality Authority, established in October 1999, has been charged with the task of promoting equality of opportunity across a wide range of areas, and monitoring progress. The absence to date of systematic data to establish benchmarks from which future progress can be targeted and monitored is likely to significantly hamper developments, and there is an urgent need to establish data-gathering mechanisms in these areas. In the case of students with disabilities, the Points Commission estimates that between 1,200 and 1,500 people, participate annually in third-level education, but there is no information on the participation of such groups in further or Adult Education generally. For Travellers, there were 414 Travellers in second-level education for whom additional resources were claimed in the 1998/99 school year. In addition, there are an estimated 740 Travellers aged 15+ participating in education and training in the network of Senior Traveller Training Centres, and an extra 135 on the Youthreach programme for early school leavers. However, data are not available in relation to other Adult Education programmes, adult literacy or third-level programmes. The Higher Education Equality Unit in its publication *Doing It Differently! Addressing Racism and Discrimination in Higher Education in Ireland 1999* indicated that out of a population of 24,000 Travellers in Ireland, only 5 participated in third-level education in 1998.

In relation to people with disabilities, a number of steps has been taken to integrate services into mainstream provision, including the establishment of a National Disability Authority. These are set out under Section 8.11 of this Paper.

1.7 Tackling Poverty

The *National Anti-Poverty Strategy (NAPS) (1997)* set out a number of goals to be achieved up to 2007.   Chief among those objectives was the global poverty reduction target of significantly reducing consistent poverty[1]   from 9-15% of households to less than 5-10% of households. For the period 1994-1997, the ESRI has shown that in the context of rising wealth and falling rates of unemployment, consistent poverty levels are being significantly reduced. In response, the Government has set a new target of reducing it to below 5% by 2004.

1.7.1 The Green Paper drew attention to the emphasis which the NAPS had accorded to education in addressing poverty and disadvantage, particularly in issues concerning early school leaving; second- chance and community education opportunities; the development of integrated, area-based services in tackling educational disadvantage and the provision of relevant guidance and counselling services in education and employment.

1.7.2 The Green Paper also drew attention to the role that Adult Education can play in addition to school in breaking the cycle of intergenerational poverty. As the foregoing tables have shown, the weaknesses of early education systems in equalising educational attainment between socio-economic groups, as opposed to simply providing equal access continue to be a source of deep concern. The Government will continue to support the early school system with additional resources to counter educational underachievement within school. Recognising, however, that parental levels of education exert a critical influence on children's participation in education and their school performance, there is an increasingly compelling case for investment in the education of parents also.   Adult Education, particularly the Community Education strand, can play a crucial role in breaking the cycle of intergenerational poverty through targeted interventions with vulnerable parents.

1.8 Catering for diversity

Uniform, nationally organised education systems find it difficult to respond to the needs of particular sub-groups. In the Irish case this is well illustrated in the case of Travellers, our biggest single minority group, who tend to experience the greatest difficulties in successfully negotiating the education system.

1.8.1 Respect for diversity around a shared identity is the challenge of inter-culturalism. The challenges that this poses to education are immense, including:-

- modes of teacher selection and training;

- language;

---

1. Consistent poverty is defined as being below 50/60% of average household disposable income and experiencing enforced basic deprivation. Basic deprivation is the presence of at least one of a list of eight indicators determined by survey to be basic necessities by, and possessed by, a majority of those surveyed. Examples include having two pairs of strong shoes, having a warm waterproof overcoat, and having a roast meal or equivalent at least once a week.

- modes of interaction and nature of

- inter-relationships between tutor and learner;

- curricula;

- course materials;

- extra-curricular activities.

1.8.2 With regard to Adult Education the challenges of inter-culturalism include:

- recognition that many immigrants, particularly refugees and asylum seekers, have specific urgent requirements, from basic information through to language training;

- the fact that many refugees and asylum seekers may not have the requisite job market skills or may have difficulty in achieving recognition for qualifications;

- recognition that many minority groups, such as Travellers or people with disabilities, may also have distinct cultural patterns which must be acknowledged in an educational context;

- the need to develop mechanisms to support different groups in ways which are empathetic to and which respect, their own heritage and cultural diversity;

- the need to provide specific tailored programmes and basicliteracy and language education for all immigrants as an elementary part of provision;

- the acknowledgement that the indigenous population also needs educational support as it adapts to an inter-cultural context;

- recognition of awards and qualifications achieved in other countries;

- the need to provide mechanisms whereby all minority and marginalised groups have the possibility to influence policy and to shape interventions which have bearing upon them;

- the need to build structures which are predicated upon the requirements of a diverse population as opposed to a uniform one, and the development of educational curricula, resources and materials, training and inservice strategies, modes of assessment and delivery methods which accept such diversity as the norm.

1.8.3 There are now over 100 different nationalities in Irish primary schools. Clearly, Ireland is rapidly evolving as a multi-racial society. Recognising the importance of this issue for the future direction of Irish society, aiming to maximise the gains of multiculturalism and pre-empting the rise of racism in Ireland, inter-culturalism will be the third underpinning principle of Government policy on Adult Education. Accordingly, all programmes supported or publicly funded will be required to demonstrate their openness and contribution to Ireland's development as an inter-cultural society.

The Government recognises that for many in Ireland involved in education generally and in Adult Education specifically, this is a new field of concern. Nonetheless, the work of non-governmental organisations involved for instance in Third World activity or with refugees and asylum seekers and with Travellers already constitutes a significant reservoir of expertise and progressive thinking which could be of great benefit to educational planners in shaping their agendas for an inter-cultural future.

1.9 Irish Language and Culture

1.9.1 In many senses there has been a major renewal of Irish cultural forms in recent years. Irish traditional music, Irish dance and writing through the medium of Irish have both flourished in an Irish context and received ever-increasing international acclaim.

A concern with this area within a lifelong learning and Adult Education framework would particularly and primarily focus on the issue of generalised participation in these forms of artistic expression and on the contribution of such activities to an enriching personal and community life as well as to a strengthening of the links to the vast Irish diaspora.

Within the broad ambit of Irish cultural concerns, the issue of Irish as a spoken language has tended to predominate. Within the context of this White Paper, Irish as a spoken language concerns:-

- Gaeltacht communities

- those not in Gaeltacht regions who speak Irish as a preferred first language and those who would wish to so do.

1.9.2 With regard to Gaeltacht communities, the Government is concerned to ensure that Gaeltacht residents have the same opportunities as are open to English speakers to pursue their education and training ambitions in their own language.

With regard to those who speak Irish as their preferred first language and those who wish to speak it, the overall positive attitude to the language, testified to in several studies, gives grounds for some optimism. Despite such positive attitudes, it is a matter of great regret that many who wish to speak Irish cannot do so.

1.9.3 Notwithstanding the excellent work of the statutory and voluntary bodies who are engaged in the promotion of the Irish language, it appears that there has been relatively little engagement between these bodies and the generality of Adult Education activity in the country. The capacity of the latter sector both to capitalise on its pedagogical innovation and to reach constituencies which the more specialised Irish language organisations are less likely to do, suggest that such an engagement would now be desirable. This White Paper will provide for opportunities for these parts of the Adult and Community Education sector, which have heretofore been largely uninvolved in Irish language or cultural education, to do so.

1.10 Conclusion

This chapter has set out a vision for the role of Adult Education in society, and the principles which should underpin its provision. It has presented an overview of participation and educational attainment levels of those aged 16-64, highlighting various issues concerning the progress of specific groups. Low levels of literacy and poor education levels, particularly among older adults, continue to pose fundamental challenges for Ireland in maintaining competitiveness and growth, and in promoting social inclusion. Adult Education has a key role to play in meeting this challenge.

Chapter2
The Policy Context

CHAPTER 2
The Policy Context

2.1 A series of international and national policy commitments and initiatives over the last ten years, coupled with the emergence of a dynamic and energetic Adult Education sector in the country, have resulted in a growing conviction at all levels of society, including Government, not merely of the desirability of large scale public investment in Adult Education, but of its necessity.

In shaping a policy, a number of aspects must be borne in mind. Firstly, even in the context of a currently favourable budgetary situation, the Government must be strategic in its investment decisions concerning Adult Education. The main strategic choice which it must make is that between developing a comprehensive framework of provision which would lay down a foundation and structure for the development of Adult Education in the country in a strategic and targeted manner, as opposed to publicly funding a mass programme of provision. This White Paper has opted for the former approach on the basis that a framework of provision which is co-ordinated within itself; integrated with the other sectors and which provides for progressive ease of movement between education/home/work is a necessary condition for the realisation of the second option - i.e. a mass programme of provision.

The White Paper recognises, however, that even where an elaborate and comprehensive system is in place, targeted interventions will be necessary so as to encourage and support the participation of some priority groups in Adult Education. In particular the Government is concerned to support those with literacy problems, with low levels of formal education (i.e. incomplete second-level), social welfare recipients, and people on low incomes in returning to education.

2.2 This White Paper, therefore, confirms the Government's commitment to the establishment of a national policy for lifelong learning and specifically to the establishment of a well-funded Adult Education system in the country.

The development of this position has been marked by a number of significant milestones and/or influences. Organisations like the European Commission, OECD and UNESCO uniformly promote lifelong learning as the foundation for education and training policy.

2.3 In Ireland, lifelong learning emerged as a central theme in the *Report of the Commission on Adult Education (1984)*. However, it was to have little impact on an education system already straining to cope with a greatly expanded provision for a rapidly increasing youth population and the financial crises of the mid-1980s. This led the OECD (1991).to conclude that, despite considerable reference to the ideal of lifelong learning and second-chance education in the Report of the Commission, in Ireland, as in *"nearly all other countries, there is no evidence of any concerted efforts to render it a reality"*

2.4 While the White Paper on Education, *Charting Our Education Future (1995)*, referred to the need to promote *"lifelong learning and continuous retraining and updating of skills"* (p.79), its main concern was with education as a front loading process or as a preparation for life.

2.5 The EU Commission marked the Year of Lifelong Learning (1996) with the publication of the *Strategy for Lifelong Learning*. Here, the Commission advanced the case for lifelong learning on a variety of grounds but focused, in particular, on the institutional and policy challenges posed by a lifelong learning commitment, particularly in issues such as the transition between place of work and place of education; progression; accreditation and tutor training.

2.6 *Lifelong Learning for All (OECD, 1996)* drew attention to the role of educational institutions, in particular, in supporting the individual's educational progress through the life cycle.

2.7 The Government *White Paper on Human Resource Development (1997)* emphasised the comparatively low levels of education of Irish adults within an OECD context and referred to the negative economic and labour market implications of such a situation if it were to remain unaddressed. Equally, it drew attention to the likely decline in the numbers exiting second-level education over the following decade and the implications which this had for sourcing skilled labour from adults not currently in the workforce and for upskilling those already in it.

2.8 The *OECD's International Adult Literacy Survey (1997)* drew attention to the particularly high rates of literacy problems in Ireland by comparison with all other countries in the study, with the exception of Poland. This study illustrated and focused attention on the significant mismatch in the resources being allocated to adult literacy provision and the scale of the task.. While the study showed that younger adults were less likely to experience literacy problems then older ones, even young adults in Ireland did not fare well relative to other countries, implying significant questions about the early school experience of children, currently. The literacy issue, both in schools and for adults, is now the focus of new Government initiatives arising out of the National Development Plan. These initiatives are highlighted in Chapter 4.

2.9 Alongside publications such as these, the Adult Education sector was itself advancing on many fronts. Statutory programmes such as State funded out-of-school Youthreach and VTOS programmes; European Commission Community Initiatives (particularly Employment NOW, YOUTHSTART, INTEGRA and HORIZON; LEADER and the Local Urban and Rural Development programme); a burgeoning - if under-funded - literacy movement; a dynamic community-based women's education sector and new developments in a greatly expanded training provision for unemployed people combined with traditional night class provision to give a whole new character and relevance to the Adult Education sector in the 1990s. In particular, the potential of this sector to combat disadvantage became increasingly evident.

2.10 These themes were taken up in the Government Green Paper, which aimed to set down the parameters of public discussion and consultation leading to the publication of a Government White Paper on Adult Education. The Green Paper has already played a major role in concentrating attention on the Adult Education sector in terms both of its centrality in shaping a national lifelong learning agenda as well as the specific potential contribution of the sector in combating disadvantage; in breaking the cycle of intergenerational poverty; in personal and cultural development activities and in enhancing national competitiveness.

2.11 DEVELOPMENTS SINCE THE GREEN PAPER

2.11.1 There has been a number of significant initiatives and developments both of direct and indirect impact on Adult Education in Ireland since the publication of the Green Paper. These have culminated in the conclusion of the national agreement published in the *Programme for Prosperity and Fairness (2000)* in which lifelong learning is a central theme.

The *NESC Report, Opportunities, Challenges and Capacities for Choice (1999)* places a major emphasis on the centrality of lifelong learning in the social and economic development strategy of the country. It adopts the EU Employment and Labour Market Committee's definition of lifelong learning as:-

> *"....All purposeful learning activity, whether formal or informal, undertaken on an ongoing basis with the aim of improving knowledge, skills and competence."* (p.170)

While it acknowledges the importance of lifelong learning for improving employability and adaptability, it considers lifelong learning to be *"essential for personal fulfilment outside the labour market as well"*. *(P.210)*

The Council makes a range of recommendations concerning lifelong learning, including:

- an active role for the social partners in promoting lifelong learning;

- the development of early childhood provision;

White Paper on Adult Education – Learning for Life

- the need to tackle high dropout rates at second-level and high attrition rates at third-level;

- intensified efforts to increase the participation of women in apprenticeship courses;

- the need to tackle the adult literacy problem;

- promoting the improved system of certification and accreditation proposed in the recently enacted *Qualifications (Education and Training) Act (1999)*, and the associated expansion of progression pathways;

- the need to promote language training;

- the need for workplace education for promoting the adaptability and employability of firms and employees;

- a recognition of the dynamic nature of the requirements of national competitiveness, involving continuous and multifaceted adjustments and refinements, but fundamentally involving two related issues in the period ahead - the information society and lifelong learning;

- a process of modernising work organisation based on common ownership of the resolution of challenges, involving the direct participation of employees/ representatives and investment in their training, development and working environment;

- progress with regard to childcare and parental leave.

2.11.2 The *Qualifications (Education and Training) Act (1999)* referred to above provides for the establishment of a National Qualifications Authority of Ireland to develop a national qualifications framework for non-university education and training awards at further and higher levels. The Authority will have the following objectives:

- to establish and maintain a framework for the development, recognition and award of qualifications in the State, based on standards of knowledge, skill and competence to be acquired by the learners;

- to establish the policies and criteria on which the framework shall be based;

- to provide a system for co-ordinating and comparing education and training awards;

- to maintain and enhance the standards of further and higher education and training awards;

- to promote and facilitate access, transfer and progression.

The Act also provides for the establishment of two councils, the Further Education and Training Awards Council (FETAC) and the Higher Education and Training Awards Council (HETAC). The roles of the Councils, at their respective levels, are to determine the standards of knowledge skill or competence to be acquired by learners; to establish and publish the policies and criteria for the making of awards and the validation of programmes; to make or recognise awards; to monitor and evaluate the quality of programmes.

The Act provides for an all-embracing network of relationships between providers in the further and higher education and training sectors, including a legislative requirement on the universities to co-operate with the new structures.

In so far as the National Qualifications Authority of Ireland provides for an overriding framework of certification and progression both within and between education and training, it is arguably one of the most important single elements in a national system of lifelong learning. It can provide for a transparent and progressive ladder of qualifications, whereby the learner can negotiate a certified learning route via a combination of providers from foundation level through to degree.

2.11.3 *The National Development Plan 2000-2006* was published by Government in November 1999 and sets out an integrated programme of education, training, and infrastructural measures to promote social inclusion, employment, competitiveness and growth, environmental sustainability and regional balance. Of particular significance within an Adult Education context is:

- the **Early Education** (£74m), **School Completion** (£75.5m), **Early Literacy** (£11.75m) and **Traveller Education** (£9.8m) measures which target disadvantage in pre-school and early education, and are designed to improve participation rates to completion of senior cycle second-level education;

- the **National Adult Literacy Strategy** (£73.8m);

- the **Further Education Support Measure** which provides £35m for programme development and the establishment, for the first time, of an Adult Educational Guidance Service in this sector;

White Paper on Adult Education – Learning for Life

- the £1.027bn investment in a **Back to Education Initiative** which will provide for a substantial expansion of part-time options across PLC, Youthreach/Traveller and VTOS programmes allied with the continuation of existing options;

- the £95m **Third-Level Access Measure** involving a range of initiatives at higher education level including:-

  - greater flexibility and college-based outreach and support programmes for students from disadvantaged backgrounds and second-chance mature students;

  - supports for students with disabilities;

  - an exploration of the role of community-based access initiatives;

  - additional financial supports for students at the lowest income levels.

- £35m for the development of a **National Qualifications Framework**

- £19.6m for a range of **equality initiatives**. These include the establishment of a dedicated Equality Unit within the Department of Education and Science to co-ordinate and monitor gender equity at all levels of the system, a computerised management information system for the Further Education sector to enable the progress of specific groups to be tracked more effectively, and expansion of the Women's Education Initiative allied with the inclusion of a strand to cater for disadvantaged men.

These developments are allied with investment in **capital** at every level of the system, a £550m third-level **Research, Technological Development and Innovation** budget, and measures to support staff development and enhanced quality and monitoring arrangements. They are complemented by increased investment in childcare under the measures co-ordinated by the Department of Justice, Equality and Law Reform.

2.11.4 The initiatives relating to educational disadvantage mentioned above, together with further developments in primary and special education and school attendance, were set out in a £194m package of measures to address disadvantage entitled *The New Deal - A Plan for Educational Opportunity* launched in December 1999. The programme sets out investment in a range of areas at every level of the system, from early childhood through to adult literacy and third-level education, to take place over the period 2000-2002.

The **Commission on the Points System** was established by the Minister for Education and Science in October 1997 and published the *Final Report and Recommendations* at the end of 1999. While the Commission reported on all aspects of third-level entry, part of its brief was to consider access to third-level of non-standard students, e.g.mature students.

The Commission has put forward a comprehensive range of proposals regarding mature students in Higher Education, dealt with comprehensively in Chapter 7, incorporating matters concerning mature student quotas; modes of delivery of third-level programmes; access courses and support services to mature students in Higher Education. It recommends that participation of mature students in third-level education should reach 15% by 2005 and 25% by 2015.

2.11.5 The *Report of the Review Committee on Post-Secondary Education and Training Places (1999)* draws attention to the rapid expansion of Higher Education in Ireland over the past three decades.

The Report, however, also draws attention to the comparatively low levels of upper second-level attainment of the Irish population aged 25-64, recognising that *"it is significantly below the OECD average"*.

The Report notes that the Leaving Certificate is still the critical gateway for further and higher education and training. Accordingly, it suggests that the ways whereby adult learners can either access Leaving Certificate or have alternative qualifications for access need to be addressed. It notes that current third-level endeavours to open up new ways of access:-

> *". . . should be strongly supported (and) . . . be accompanied by a systematic widening of the recognition accorded for entry purposes to other types of national award . . . . we consider that increased flexibility, including the optimum use of part-time and distance learning, workplace delivery and greater emphasis on mechanisms for the accreditation of prior learning and work-based experience will be essential in making provision for mature students." (P.60/61)*

The Report takes the view that there is scope for increasing third-level participation for mature students, and recommends an *additional* stock of 10,000 places for mature students, predominantly part-time, to be built up over a number of years. It proposes that institutions, including all those providing distance education opportunities in the State should be encouraged to develop a strategy for increasing adult access and participation.

2.11.6 The *White Paper on Early Childhood Education, Ready to Learn (1999)*, identifies the principal objective of Government policy in regard to early childhood education as supporting:-

"the development and educational achievement of children through high quality early education, with particular focus on the target groups of the disadvantaged and those with special needs" (p.14)

The White Paper locates this commitment within an overall concern for lifelong learning, noting a shift in emphasis in recent years from a singular focus in education on schools and third-level institutions *"towards a continuum of lifelong learning"*.

The White Paper proposes a comprehensive strategy for the development of a system of early childhood education. Apart from the overall beneficial impact of such a development in terms of its long-term contribution towards improving the overall levels of educational attainment of Irish adults, the White Paper's emphasis on supporting parental involvement in early childhood education is also welcome from an Adult Education point of view.

The Paper draws attention to the central educational role which parents play in the child's early development; to the value of two-way communication between parents and the formal pre-school and school system and also to the benefits which parents derive from such an involvement. It goes on to outline a multi-faceted strategy to facilitate parental involvement including:

- a strategy of greater provision in the home through a combination of financial support and more flexible working arrangements;

- supporting the establishment of mobile units with equipment, materials and books;

- the provision of parenting courses building on existing provision for Adult Education and on courses run in the private sector and by community and umbrella groups;

- further research on best practice in parental involvement (p.115-117).

2.11.7 *A Report by the Information Society Commission: Building a Capacity for Change –* *Lifelong Learning in the Information Society* was published in July 1999. Its key recommendations focus on:-

- critical attention to preventing early school leaving;

- optimising the use and relevance of ICT in teaching and learning, together with investment in technical support, teacher training and curriculum development, and supported by low cost Internet access;

- increased investment in adult literacy using new technology to the full;

- a national adult ICT literacy initiative, building partnerships with education and training institutions, media organisations, libraries, and schools;

- further development of the work of the Expert Group on Future Skills Needs;

- speedy implementation of the National Qualifications Framework including the development of mechanisms for the accreditation of prior learning and work-based learning;

- improved responsiveness and flexibility among education and training providers to meet clients' needs, including a focus on capacity-building and awareness-raising among communities, groups and individuals to stimulate demand for lifelong learning;

- increased investment in training by Irish business;

- incentives to promote individual investment in education and training;

- investment in libraries to enable them to play a key role as centres for community access to ICT resources and learning in the Information Age.

2.11.8 Lifelong learning is a central theme of the *Programme for Prosperity and Fairness 2000* which sets out a comprehensive range of actions aimed at promoting Ireland's capacity as a socially inclusive knowledge-based society, which is adaptable to change. Framework 4 sets out an integrated set of measures within the context of a continuum from early childhood through to adulthood. These include preventing

White Paper on Adult Education – Learning for Life

and addressing early school leaving; addressing literacy needs; promoting technology, science and languages; addressing barriers to access and progression of specific groups; enhancing participation in second-chance, adult and third-level education and training; addressing blockages in apprenticeship training; and promoting the community dimension of education and training. The enhancement of employment services ; the development of an educational adult guidance service; the promotion of family-friendly policies; and the development and expansion of childcare facilities form part of the approach.

2.11.9 The *National Employment Action Plan 2000* sets out a comprehensive framework for effective labour market reform to support economic and employment growth and a reduction in social exclusion. Under Guidelines 1 and 2 of the Plan, an activation strategy is being implemented to provide systematic guidance, counselling and support, placement in education, training or a work experience programme, or placement in employment for all persons entering a critical stage in their unemployment. The Strategy was introduced on 1 September 1998 targeted at unemployed young people under 25 approaching their sixth month of unemployment, and has been expanded on a phased basis since then. The objective is to extend the process in 10-year age groups to all adults who are unemployed by mid-2000. The activation strategy is being implemented by the FÁS Employment Services in collaboration with the Department of Social, Community and Family Affairs. It is supported by a strengthening of investment in the Employment Services, and a growth in flexible opportunities to return to training, including a rapid expansion in Bridging Measures, and increased targeting of the long-term unemployed under the FÁS Action Plan for Long-term Unemployed. Key priorities are to address skill and labour shortages through assisting the unemployed to return to work, increasing labour force participation (particularly females and older workers), and developing a balanced immigration policy to meet specific skills. Promotion of lifelong learning opportunities, expansion of e-commerce, and upskilling of those in the workplace form important elements of the approach.

2.11.10 The *Education (Welfare) Act 2000* raises the school-leaving age to 16, or completion of lower second-level education, whichever is the later, and makes provision for the establishment of an Educational Welfare Board to monitor school attendance and support children at risk to stay in school. The Act also provides for the registration with the Educational Welfare Board of young people aged between 16 and 18 years who intend to leave school early. The Board will draw up a plan for the further education and training of the individual, and will require that the person concerned make all reasonable efforts to carry out the plan. It is on this basis that the Board will issue a certificate entitling the young person to work. It will not be possible for a young person aged between 16 and 18 years to be employed without a certificate. A total of £4.25 million is being allocated over the next three years for the initial establishment of the Board and the implementation of the Bill when enacted.

The implementation of the Act will have a critical impact, not only on promoting improved retention rates in school, but also on ensuring a systemic approach to tracking, outreach and referral arrangements for early school leavers to further education. As such it will play an important part in enhancing the effectiveness of programmes such as Youthreach which, although highly successful in catering for clients who join the programme, currently lack the investment of specific resources for tracking, outreach and initial contact work. The focus of the Educational Welfare Boards on those aged 16-18 who have left school will also pose key challenges for the education and training sector in developing appropriate and flexible responses to enable this group to continue their learning.

2.12 Conclusion

This Chapter sets out the national and international policy reports which set the context for developments in Adult Education. Even in the short period since the publication of the Green Paper, it is clear from a range of Government actions and official publications that there is an emerging national consensus on the urgency of an expanded Adult Education system and on the key issues which such a system should address. These issues were further articulated in the consultation process following the publication of the Green Paper, addressed in the next Chapter.

Chapter3
The Consultation
Process

CHAPTER 3
The Consultation Process

3.1 GREEN PAPER ON ADULT EDUCATION

3.1.1 The Government Green Paper on Adult Education was published in November 1998. The purpose of the Green Paper was:-

- to begin a national debate and inform Government policy with regard to the key role of Adult Education in meeting the challenges confronting this society currently;

- to set out a basis for a national policy on Adult Education and to identify priorities;

- to propose mechanisms for the co-ordination of this sector within an holistic and inclusive system of education and within an overall national policy commitment to lifelong learning.

It is not the intention here to revisit in any great detail the rationale or the specific proposals of the Green Paper. However, insofar as the Green Paper is the essential backdrop to the thinking and recommendations of this White Paper, it is useful to restate its main elements.

The Green Paper presented a profile of the educational attainment of Irish adults as one which declined significantly with age and which compared unfavourably with most countries in the industrialised world. In particular, it drew attention to the nature and extent of the literacy problem in the Irish adult population, and to the consequences of low levels of educational attainment in terms of problems of poverty, unemployment, intergenerational disadvantage and the relative competitiveness of the workforce.

3.1.2 The Green Paper went on to propose a range of initiatives, within a lifelong learning framework, to deal with these issues, proposing:-

- a multi-faceted National Adult Literacy programme;

- the establishment of a Back to Education Initiative, incorporating wider and part-time access to Youthreach and Traveller programmes, PLCs and VTOS;

- a commitment to upskilling the workforce, particularly in building a closer relationship between the world of work and that of education and through a system of paid educational leave;

- a range of proposals aimed at increasing mature student participation in Higher Education, including the contribution of distance education;

- a recognition of the unique and innovative contribution of the community education sector, particularly of community-based women's education;

- a series of proposals concerning outcomes-based assessment; certification of education and training and progression within and between them;

- a system of adult guidance and counselling;

- a system of tutor training and recognition of qualifications;

- widely representative, inclusionary structures at national and local level for the co-ordination and development of Adult Education and training.

3.2 THE CONSULTATION PROCESS

3.2.1 Alongside the written submissions, organisations with a national or sector- wide remit were also invited to make oral submissions to Department officials to elaborate on the written position papers and to highlight particular matters to which they wished to draw attention. During the summer of 1999 about seventy groups engaged in individual meetings with the Department. These included education and training providers, national community and voluntary sector interests, trade union and employer bodies, research organisations, Government Departments, and organisations representing the needs of specific groups.

Paralleling this process, the Department itself convened six regional consultative meetings throughout the country in the early summer of 1999. More than four hundred practitioners, providers and learners participated in these seminars.

The consultation process concluded with a one-day Forum in Dublin Castle on September 22nd 1999 at which the main issues to emerge in the consultation process were relayed back to the participants, focusing in particular on those aspects of the Green Paper over which there had been some disagreement or dissension in the course of the consultation process.

3.2.2 It is not possible in the context of this publication to do justice to the range, comprehensiveness or detail that emerged in this extensive process. While cognisant of the risks of generalising, the main summative insights from the process were:-

- widespread welcome for the Green Paper both in its perceived timeliness, in its priorities and in its policy proposals;

- a view that the White Paper should reflect the overall direction and emphasis of the Green Paper;

- a recognition that the Green Paper had furthered the emergence of a national policy on lifelong learning, and that this was the most appropriate framework within which to approach a policy on Adult Education;

- that a lifelong emphasis raised the issue of the early school experience as a valid concern of the Adult Education sector;

- a concern that issues of socio-economic status and gender, equality and inter-culturalism should implicitly underpin all Adult Education policy initiatives;

- that the policy objectives for Adult Education should equally embrace personal, cultural and social goals as well as economic ones;

- arising from the fee structure and difficulties with childcare, issues of differential access for several groups were prominent throughout the consultation;

- a concern that the particular role of Adult Education in areas such as the Irish language, the arts and complementary therapies which had received little attention in the Green Paper be elaborated upon in the White Paper and that the North/South dimension be emphasised;

- a concern that the needs of marginalised groups such as prisoners, the elderly, people with disabilities, Travellers and other minorities are uppermost in the White Paper;

- concerns with problems of transport for people in rural areas;

- a view that the enormous potential of ICT be recognised as a means for widening access to information and education on a previously unprecedented scale.

Such generalised positions, of course, gave rise to many detailed recommendations and proposals throughout the process. Many of these have been adopted within the strictures of Government budgetary policy and with reference to the occasionally different positions of some of the stakeholders.

3.3 Lifelong Learning

There was a widespread welcome in the consultation process for the lifelong learning emphasis in the Green Paper and in the location of Adult Education policy themes within the emergence of a lifelong learning focus in policy, especially at European level. Generally, it was felt that the lifelong learning emphasis gave a coherence and a framework to the concept of a continuum of learning from the cradle to the grave. Additionally, it strengthened the arguments against a singular focus on the front-loading of education and legitimised arguments for progression, credit accumulation, diversification of provision and flexible routeways between home/work and education.

Despite such attractions, however, there was also a view that the lifelong learning theme could have been extended further in the Paper. In particular, it was pointed out that a lifelong learning focus should concern itself much more with the early school experience, particularly with that of school under-achievement. Some commentators referred to the *hermetic nature* of the different educational sectors/levels in Ireland, giving rise to little inter-sectoral learning in areas such as methodologies and a continuous tendency in the early school years to seek in-school solutions to what may be out-of-school problems. Further, it was felt that lifelong should not be limited to the work-based lifespan but should recognise the learning needs and potential contribution of older learners.

3.4 Marginalised Groups

3.4.1 The Green Paper drew attention to the range of statutory and non-statutory driven programmes for those who were educationally or otherwise disadvantaged. Many of the submissions on the Green Paper came from organisations in the non-statutory sector and NGO groups working with the marginalised in society. Perhaps the defining character of many of these organisations - though, not all - was the extent to which they were both in and of the marginalised. In essence, then, they transcended the divide between the provider and the learner, embodying the twin aspects of community education referred to in the Green Paper as a *programme* and *an approach*.

There was a general concern that a focus on marginalisation required a coherent and comprehensive commitment to equality and inter-culturalism in all programmes. Women's interests were particularly concerned in this regard, pointing out that a reliance on labour market data obscured the position of women not in the labour force and indeed was likely to miss the gender-based disadvantages of women in the workforce also, a matter already addressed in the opening Chapter.

3.4.2 In general, the submissions from marginalised groups shared a number of common themes. These included:-

(a) A view of social exclusion as a phenomenon not merely of poverty but as a structural process of disablement, whereby disadvantaged groups are both rendered voiceless and powerless.

"What is done without us is against us"

(African proverb cited by Irish Deaf Society)

Such an analysis gives a particular character to the Adult Education approach to disadvantage - notions of communal and group empowerment as opposed to individualised interventions tend to predominate in proposed initiatives. Groups from the disability area also tended to emphasise *entitlement* rather than *concession* in their proposals.

(b) In some instances, excluded groups seeing themselves as cohesive minority groups - i.e. groups actively discriminated against by the daily practices normalised in the wider society. Groups such as the deaf, Travellers and other minority groups were particularly likely to see themselves in this way.

(c) The fact that, generally the marginalised groups who made submissions were receiving funding and other supports from a wide range of agencies and sources. Many had benefited from the various EU initiatives, particularly the Employment (HORIZON, INTEGRA, YOUTHSTART and NOW) initiatives, and the Global Grants for Local Development as well as from a variety of Government departments and State agencies.

(d) Endorsement of the recognition accorded to the Community Education sector in the Green Paper. The CORI submission, for instance, noted that it was:

"extremely significant that the Green Paper recognises Community Education as an area for which a policy framework needs to be developed as part of policy development in education generally" (p.27)

Similarly, AONTAS also noted the recognition accorded to the sector and suggested that its development be supported by the appointment of Community Resource Workers.

(e) A strong concern throughout the sector that it be adequately represented in national and local structures.

(f) The theme of innovation in formulating new and effective bottom-up educational strategies within marginalised groups. Sabel (1996) has noted the innovation of such groups when he drew attention to the capacity of local development groups throughout the country to generate successful new solutions to local problems, while he also raised the difficulties of the statutory sector in mainstreaming such innovations.

There was general support, therefore, for the positioning of the Green Paper in endorsing such creativity; in recognising that it needed mainstreaming for its long-term security, but that such mainstreaming should not be achieved at the expense of such creativity. The "long arm of the State" was something about which many groups were concerned.

(g) The fact that recognition accorded to Community Education would have to include the validation of the learning in such groups in ways which:

(h) enhanced the co-operative communal aspect of Community Education as opposed to an individualistic, competitive character;

(i) engaged the expertise of local activists;

(j) acknowledged the unique ability of those community groups to reach hard-to-reach audiences with personnel drawn from the self-same areas or groups. This tended to raise the possibility of such groups taking a more orthodox provider role on behalf of statutory organisations who may have no physical presence in such communities or who simply find it hard to engage highly marginalised people in their activities. The potential contribution of such an approach in areas such as literacy provision; in engaging with disadvantaged men; in working with the elderly; or in working with people with disabilities in providing vocational courses on behalf of statutory bodies, all emerge as possible areas of development.

3.4.3 Overall, key concerns expressed related to the degree of emphasis given to the needs of specific groups within the Green Paper, particularly in relation to women, Travellers, people with disabilities, prisoners, refugees and asylum seekers. It was argued that:-

- the needs of specific groups, and the barriers that face them must be named explicitly;

- an equality strategy and proofing tools are needed for each group;

- there is both a need for tailor-made positive action programmes to address specific needs, and a mechanism to ensure access to mainstream at every level;

- progress must be benchmarked and tracked through systematic auditing, equality proofing and data monitoring. The lack of data on the participation of particular groups was highlighted as a key deficiency in the development of an equality proofing strategy.

3.4.4 In regard to prison education, the need was highlighted for recognition and further investment in this area, as well as improved linkages and an integrated approach linking the work within prison to progression and support for prisoners on their release. This raises issues for the education of prisoners themselves, and for appropriate mechanisms for a family-based approach, such as that developed under the Dillon's Cross project as part of the Women's Education Initiative.

3.4.5 In relation to people with disabilities, the absence to date of a specific focus within Further Education in meeting their needs was highlighted, and criticisms were expressed that the strategies proposed in the Green Paper focused almost entirely on the needs of those with physical disabilities, and did not provide for those with learning difficulties.

For Community Education, the responses focused on the need for specific proposals to develop the sector and highlighted 3 Rs - recognition, resources and representation. In particular, the need for a separate budget line within the education system was highlighted, allied with mechanisms to promote and nurture the sector's development while retaining its unique philosophy and processes of engagement and delivery.

3.5 Issues for Providers: Self-financed Part-time Adult Education

3.5.1 The *lifewide* dimension of Adult Education implies a multiplicity of learning sites and education providers. Naturally, organisations whose primary purpose is education were most prominent here. Submissions were received from a total of 16 VECs as well as from their co-ordinating organisation, the IVEA, the Teachers' Union of Ireland and the Association of Chief Executive Officers of the VECs. Submissions were also received from the voluntary secondary sector through the JMB and ASTI and also from the Association of Community and Comprehensive Schools and the National Association of Community Education Directors. Clearly the entirety of the second-level sector utilised the Green Paper to engage in an in-depth analysis of their respective roles and future in Adult Education.

Generally, many of the providers were working in an environment where adults were not the primary target or their core mission. While all recognised that working with adults enhanced their work with young people, in operational terms it was not always easy to reconcile the needs of both sets of learners. In particular, it was pointed out that the day-school tended to have first call on premises and facilities and, even where these buildings and facilities were available, they were not necessarily adult-friendly in design or culture.

3.5.2 Specific issues, which preoccupied this body of providers, included:-

1. the existence of inadequate resources within the sector which would enable it to pursue a comprehensive programme of Adult Education. Resource deficiencies affected all aspects of delivery but mainly included:-

   - difficulties in utilising day-school facilities for night-class purposes;

   - inadequate provision for caretaking, secretarial and promotional support, especially in schools that were attempting to develop an Adult Education programme;

   - high rental charges on buildings;

   - loss of day-school teaching hours where teachers received promotion to posts of responsibility based on night class numbers.

2. a general view that the rigid application of the self-financing principle made it particularly difficult for smaller schools in rural areas to develop a programme of Adult Education;

3.   a shared concern with the pay rates of tutors and with their career paths;

4.   a concern that in any new structures for Adult Education, all the providers would have equal representation and would have equal access to resources. Such a situation would enable a much more active involvement by the voluntary secondary sector and allow the community and comprehensive sector to develop upon an already large provision.

3.5.3 In relation to issues other than part-time self-financed programmes, the submissions concentrated on the need for investment in supporting services such as guidance, transport and childcare; a strategic focus on the development of local Adult Education teams with designated personnel; the speedy implementation of the qualifications framework; the resourcing of community education and the role and function of the proposed local and national structures. Removing financial barriers to access was also a key concern.

3.6   Adults and Higher Education

3.6.1 With regard to institutions in the Higher Education sector, the IoTs and Universities draw particular attention to:-

- the need to abolish fees for part-time students;

- the need for mechanisms to translate part-time students pursuing nationally certified courses into Full-Time Equivalent (FTE) students for funding purposes - i.e. the need to abolish the self-financing principle as applied to short extra-mural courses where candidates undertake national assessment and certification;

- a view that such courses had proven highly effective in introducing adults to university and in enabling them to move onto a ladder of progression within the higher education system;

- the desirability of incentives both to institutions and to participants to increase participation rates, especially in the higher status faculties;

- the need for continued support to institutions to institutionalise mature student-friendly processes in areas concerning access; recognition of prior learning; credit accumulation and transfer between and within institutions; and continued progress towards modularisation and semesterisation;

- the recognition that the concept of full-time/part-time student is becoming increasingly redundant as more third-level students pursue modularised, flexible study patterns. In this context, embracing a wide mature student clientele in Higher Education would presage a much more fundamental and generalised institutional reform of curricula, timetabling and modes of delivery in higher education;

- the desirability of overall national targets for participation in Higher Education and an accompanying strategic plan for the realisation of such targets.

3.6.2 There are three further points which merit mention in the discussion on Higher Education. Firstly, it was argued that immigration will mean that the number of school leavers will be higher in the coming ten years than is anticipated in the Green Paper. Demographic trends, therefore, may not favour mature student participation in Higher Education to the extent envisaged in the Green Paper.

Furthermore, the view was advanced in the consultation process that even if the numbers in the traditional cohorts of Higher Education applicants begin to fall, the current high levels of suppressed demand for university places is likely to mean that the fall will be experienced sequentially, firstly by the PLCs, then by the IoT sector: and finally by the Universities (Fitzgerald, 1999). In the absence of specific interventions, it would be left to the PLCs and the IoTs to address the task of raising mature student participation rates in Further and Higher Education.

3.6.3 A final point with regard to Higher Education concerns the issue of distance education. The potential of distance education and indeed its current contribution were perhaps understated in the Green Paper. There are possibly as many as seven thousand students taking distance education programmes in Ireland currently, primarily with Oscail and the Open University. The Oscail model has proven cost-effective and an efficient use of scarce resources. In the context of changing technology, constraints on physical capacity, the demand for localised access, the need for enhanced flexibility, adult-friendly and family-friendly policies and the need to provide for increased professional development of those in the workforce, a more pro-active and strategic approach to the development of distance learning is an imperative. The development of digital television, and the plans of RTE to provide a dedicated educational channel will also pose challenges, as well as providing increased opportunities for learners to engage at their own pace in ongoing education and training.

3.7 The Workforce

3.7.1 There was a widespread view of the Green Paper that its concern with labour market issues was excessively instrumental. While all recognised the *realpolitik* of budgetary decision-making, there was a view that arguments about national competitiveness tended to obscure the other arguments also advanced in the Green Paper about social cohesion, personal development, cultural enrichment and the critical participation in democratic structures. It was felt to be important that the broad, developmental agenda of Adult Education should not be lost sight of as the core purpose. In an area such as literacy, for instance, which received a great deal of much welcomed attention in the Green Paper, a focus on competitiveness might come to be interpreted as giving rise to narrow, functional interventions in relation to skills as opposed to the more holistic, learner-centred and developmental approaches which currently underpin literacy provision.

3.7.2 There is a developing consensus both in the field and in the literature that the traditional education/training dichotomy, if ever valid, is no longer so. An instrumental, utilitarian focus in education or training is no longer likely to be adequate to the needs of the modern worker, who increasingly requires problem solving, team work and leadership skills in a work environment requiring flexibility, adaptability and mobility. There is then an increasing convergence in the requirements of the workplace and the objectives of a broadly-based, person-centred active learning approach.

3.7.3 While, clearly, skill shortages continue to threaten Ireland's current economic prospects and there is widespread agreement amongst all stakeholders concerning its priority status, there is less agreement as to how workplace education should be organised and financed. Employers are concerned that such training should not be disruptive of the workplace and, where an expense is incurred, the employers' contribution should be discretionary - i.e. should be of a voluntary nature. Additionally, smaller employers have a concern that training can result in the loss of workers to other, sometimes bigger, employers. They are concerned that they may end up carrying the training costs of personnel who are then "poached" by larger employers. Employers were one of many other groupings who stressed the need for training in ICT, to counter exclusion and maximise its capacity as an education and training vehicle.

3.7.4 The trade unions now see investment in the workforce as a natural extension of the large-scale investment in education and training with unemployed people over the past two decades. In particular, they are concerned that the locale of educational disadvantage is now moving increasingly into low-wage, low-skilled employment in which workers may have little chance for further education or training. They are concerned that such disadvantaged workers may be least likely to benefit from an expanding provision of education and training in the workplace and will be particularly vulnerable to unemployment in the event of an economic or sectoral downturn.

3.7.5 Paid educational leave is one of their preferred means of providing ongoing education and training for the workforce. They are clear that such training should be broadly based; have identified difficulties which must be overcome in utilising the workplace as a site for literacy provision; recognise that the Trade Union movement itself can become a major provider in the lifelong learning area and see this area as part of its ongoing role in the context of the *Programme for Prosperity and Fairness (2000)*.

3.7.6 Among virtually all the responses, there was widespread criticism of the proposals in the Green Paper to maintain the fee structure for part-time third-level students, and to charge fees for non-unemployed/welfare or non-medical cardholder categories under the Back to Education Initiative. It was argued that this strategy would continue to discriminate against women in the home, and would also present barriers to a return to learning of those in work who had low skills and educational levels. Strong argument was made that "educational need" should be the critical criterion in determining who should receive State support to return to learning.

3.7.7 In regard to third-level education, it was argued that charging fees for part-time students was inconsistent with a broadly enunciated policy of enabling adults to return to learning and promoting flexibility and system change to enable people to continually upgrade their skills. Furthermore, given the scope for full-time students to engage in part-time work as a consequence of improved opportunities in the labour market, it was deemed inequitable that one category should have access to free fees and a means-tested maintenance grant, while the other should only have access to tax relief.

3.8 SUPPORT SERVICES

3.8.1 Adult Education Guidance and Counselling:

There was widespread welcome for the Green Paper's proposals regarding Adult Education guidance and counselling. There was a widespread view that information services regarding Adult Education, not to mention personalised supports in developing individual learning plans, are inadequate. There was also a view that the development of new models of outreach, which could attract those least likely to participate, was a priority.

3.8.2 Childcare/Carers

Throughout the consultation the needs of carers in accessing Adult Education were continuously emphasised. Apart from the fact that as many as 30% of all carers are over the age of sixty, the housebound nature of the care of dependent relatives - whether elderly or children - is a key area which must be addressed if access to Adult Education is to be widened. Numerous submissions stressed the issue of inadequate childcare as the major barrier to adult learning opportunities, particularly for women. While the Green Paper made several references to this issue, the consultation reinforces the view that a national childcare programme is an essential pre-requisite to the establishment of a comprehensive Adult Education programme nationally.

3.8.3 Training of Trainers

The thrust of the Green Paper with regard to the development of a cadre of professionally trained adult educators was generally welcomed in the consultation process. The general welcome was, however, tempered by a fear that such a move could prove exclusionary, not only removing the large corps of voluntary tutors from the system, but also taking some excellent practitioners who lack a tutor qualification out of the system.

It is important that professionalising the sector does not have such consequences. This would not arise if the task were approached on the more open, flexible and criteria-referenced assessment principles advocated elsewhere in the Green Paper. It would indeed be ironic if adult educators, so generally committed to breaking down barriers of academic elitism were simultaneously to construct such barriers to their own profession!

Assuming that such legitimate concerns can be overcome, the training and upgrading of Adult Education tutors is generally seen as a priority by the field. A submission from a LEONARDO Project that looked at the training needs of Further Education tutors found:

- a consensus on the need for a required minimum level of teaching/training qualifications for educators in the sector;

- the need for formal recognition of such qualifications;

- a view that the Department of Education and Science should facilitate those without a qualification to gain such a qualification.

Associated with the task of tutor training and recognition, is the issue of terms of employment and pay rates for Adult Education tutors. Many submissions in the consultation process draw attention to the contractual and temporary nature of many of those employed in the sector and to the 'modest' hourly pay rates of Adult Education tutors. It was argued that pre-tax pay rates of circa £17 per hour were proving increasingly unattractive to tutors, many of whom were working in the evening time or at other unsocial hours.

3.8.4 Transport

There was a concern amongst groups working in rural areas or in the field of disability with issues of transport to and from education and training centres. There was a particular concern that the needs of the isolated rural elderly be addressed in this regard.

3.8.5 Accreditation and Certification

Issues of concern to the field concerning accreditation and certification issues include:-

- the urgency of developing systems for the accreditation of prior learning, whether experiential or otherwise;

- a particular concern that learning undertaken in Community Education and/or the workplace would be recognised within the formal system;

- recognition of the need for flexible delivery systems and for transparent progression routeways through the education lifecycle;

- welcome for the establishment of the National Qualifications Authority of Ireland with a concern that the National Adult Learning Council has direct representation on this Authority;

- concern that accreditation and certification be approached from the perspective of the needs of the learner rather than from the requirements of the provider. This would lead to a general endorsement of the criteria-referenced, outcomes- focused approach to assessment advocated in the Green Paper.

3.9 STRUCTURES

There was no consensus in the consultation process regarding the hosting of local structures for Adult Education, although the level of attention given to this issue in the consultation process and in the submissions was less than expected. This occurred notwithstanding the fact that all the regional seminars were organised to include a specific workshop on the theme of the structures which should underpin future developments. Put simply, where disagreement emerged, it crystallised around one issue – a pro-VEC and an anti-VEC position.

The case for the VECs included:

- the fact that there is provision in the Vocational Education Act (1930) for autonomous boards within the VEC structure;

- the fact that VECs already have administrative and managerial capacity to host such boards, at minimal additional cost;

- the fact that VECs have a record of achievement and innovation in the area which could be built upon by locating the local boards within them;

- the fact that there are well-established structures for accountability within the VECs, both politically and in executive terms;

- the recognition in the IVEA published submission, *Pathways to Progress 1999,* of the validity of criticisms leveled at the *ad hoc* Adult Education Boards and proposing specific arrangements for the representation of all key stakeholders and the development of an integrated multi-agency approach.

Those who were opposed to the location of such boards within the VECs pointed to:

- the untenability of a position which argues that it is possible to have autonomy within a larger structure;

- the historical deficiencies of the *ad hoc* Adult Education Boards;

- the fact that the granting of a pre-eminent position to one provider would of necessity mitigate against equal treatment and representation for all providers.

While there was disagreement on this matter, there was nonetheless widespread agreement on other aspects concerning the functioning of such boards, particularly regarding:

- the importance of an area-based approach with agencies working together, harnessing the energy of the community and voluntary sector and prioritising the interests of the most disadvantaged;

- the integration and regulation of programmes in areas such as quality control, involvement of the learners and of the voluntary and community sector in their structures;

- the need to engage the other educational sectors within their structures so as to ensure a *lifelong* dimension for their pre-occupations;

- a role for the boards in funding the delivery of programmes and putting in place other services such as guidance and counselling within their geographic areas;

- the desirability that the local boards should report directly to the National Adult Learning Council regardless of the hosting body.

In addition, it was argued that for the local boards to be effective it would be essential to invest strategically in the development of local Adult Education teams. These could include a Director of Adult Education, programme managers, a literacy co-ordinator, guidance and information staff, staff development and curriculum support officers and administrative and technical support.

3.10 Capital

The submissions received highlighted the inadequacy of premises providing Adult Education services and the ad hoc approach to date in meeting needs in this area. They questioned the value for money of a continued focus on rental of premises as opposed to the systematic development of a network of State-owned adult and community education sites throughout the country. While falling enrolments in mainstream schools were acknowledged, it was pointed out that schools were not always eager to allow the use of their premises for Adult Education. The absence of funding mechanisms covering rental, care-taking, administrative and technical support militated against such availability; the ethos was not always conducive to adult access, and the premises often lacked facilities where adult participants could take a tea/coffee break or snack in an informal atmosphere. In addition, lack of storage facilities, accommodation for necessary day-time office staff and provision for record systems posed added barriers.

Espousing a lifelong learning policy, it was argued, was inconsistent with a building strategy which catered only for initial education within an in-school or third-level context. In addition, the need for technical support, for upgraded equipment, ICT development and networking, low-cost Internet access and facilities for community education access were all seen as a critical part of an investment strategy to support lifelong learning. Adaptation of premises to ensure suitability for use by people with disabilities, opportunities for building in greenfield sites where no premises are available for rental, and the development of a network of stand-alone Adult Education centres were all seen as important if a quality service is to be promoted.

The IVEA submission made a strong plea for capital for the establishment of Adult Education centres "which would well serve the community and could be utilised by a number of agencies for a number of purposes in the promotion, provision and delivery of programmes/courses, advice centres etc to meet the needs of adults." The development of multi-plex facilities providing for a range of community services for different needs (e.g course delivery, adult ICT access, creche, café, advice centre, guidance, youth service etc), for which a £1m budget was made available for the first time in 1999, was cited as having significant potential in providing much needed services in disadvantaged areas. The extensive network of more than 300 libraries countrywide was also noted as a major resource for adult learning purposes.

3.11 Conclusion

This Chapter sets out the feedback which provided in the comprehensive consultation process which followed publication of the *Green Paper: Adult Education in an Era of Lifelong Learning 1998*. While there was widespread welcome for the Green Paper and its priorities, the main concerns were:-

- that policy objectives should embrace personal, cultural and social goals as well as economic ones, and be seen as promoting collective as well as personal development;

- that issues of equality should underpin all education initiatives, and that the barriers to access and progression faced by specific groups should be named explicitly and strategies implemented to tackle them;

- that there was an urgent need to develop flexible mechanisms for accreditation of prior and work-based learning;

- that the role of the community education sector needed to be promoted and further strengthened;

- that charging fees for part-time third-level students and for certain categories under the Back to Education Initiative would inhibit access and present barriers for women in the home or those in the workplace with low educational levels.

Chapter 4
Second-Chance and Further Education

CHAPTER 4
Second Chance and Further Education

4.1 Consistent with its 'lifewide' commitment in the development of an Adult Education system, this White Paper has developed a range of comprehensive proposals for Adult Education in key learning sites:-

- School-based or out-of-school further education provision;

- Community;

- Workplace;

- Universities, Institutes of Technology and other third-level sites.

This Chapter deals with the first of the above, i.e. school-based or out-of-school further and second-chance education provision.

4.2 Background

In developing an all-embracing system for second-chance and Further Education in Ireland, top priorities are to address:-

- the low literacy levels of the Irish adult population already alluded to;

- the large numbers of Irish adults (1.1m aged 15-64) who have not completed upper second-level education, of whom 529,600 have not completed lower second-level.

Considerations in looking at existing provision for this population include:-

- the rigidity of the Irish education system, with its predominant emphasis on full-time provision: time specific entry and exit opportunities, and its linear, sequential organisation;

- difficulties in combining 'earning and learning' in a situation where increased job opportunities are resulting in participants being attracted out of education prior to completion of programmes;

- problems in engaging with hard-to-reach groups such as long-term unemployed males; adults with negative initial school experience; the homeless and older unemployed;

- recognition of the contribution to-date and the further potential of the existing infrastructure for second chance and further education, namely:-

Adult Literacy

Basic and Community Education provision

Youthreach

Senior Traveller Training Centres

Vocational Training Opportunities Scheme (VTOS)

Post Leaving Certificate (PLC)

Self-funded night-class provision in second-level schools and other centres.

The overall considerations in shaping a programme for the development of Second-Chance and Further Education is for:-

- an expansion of provision in line with needs;

- greater synergy between the different elements of programme provision;

- increased emphasis on successfully reaching those most in need and on expanding provision at Foundation and Level 1 or equivalent;

- flexibility and adaptation to ensure that programmes offer a wider range of choices which are appropriate to the learning, domestic and employment needs of learners.

4.3 Programme for Second-Chance and Further Education

Bearing in mind the different priority groups, current provision and overall budgetary considerations, the Government has decided to focus the development of a framework of second-chance and Further Education provision on four pillars:-

- a National Adult Literacy Programme as the top priority;

- a Back to Education Initiative (BTEI) providing for a significant expansion of part-time options under Youthreach/Traveller, VTOS and PLC courses, with a particular emphasis on promoting a return to learning of those in the population with less than upper secondary education;

- an ICT Basic Skills programme for adults as part of the Back to Education Initiative;

- increased flexibility and improved organisational structures for self-funded part-time Adult Education in schools.

In addition, as part of this process, a capital expenditure programme for Further Education will be provided, and a structural review will be undertaken of the management, organisational, administrative, technical and ancillary supports for PLC provision.

4.4 National Adult Literacy Programme

As noted earlier, the International Literacy Survey (1997) elevated concerns about the adult literacy problem to centre stage in educational policy. This was reflected in the level of attention accorded to the discussion in the Green Paper, and in the scale of resources directed to the issue since the publication of the report.

Since the launch of the OECD survey, provision for adult literacy in the education sector increased from a base of $0.85m in 1997 to $7.825m in 2000, plus an additional $0.960m for programme development. The Green Paper proposed that this level of investment be increased to at least $10m per annum, catering for the order of 15,000 clients per year.

4.4.1 As an initial step an Adult Literacy Development Fund was been established to fund a range of pilot actions which tested models and innovatory approaches to inform future practice in the area. Such initiatives concerned themselves with promoting public awareness; developing new outreach strategies for those most in need; establishing referral networks; more flexible delivery mechanisms, including group tuition.

4.4.2 Expanding and Diversifying the Programme

These initiatives, combined with a growing provision, have ensured that:-

- the clients catered for annually have increased from 5,000 to 13,000 between 1997 and early 2000;

- a range of media (church announcements, local radio, posters leaflets, past participants, outreach staff and referral networks) are used to promote the programme;

- provision includes night-time, morning and day-time classes;

- a continuum from one-to-one voluntary tuition to group work to progression to certified learning options is being developed;

- referral networks with FÁS, LES, Partnerships, Health Centres, welfare and community groups, playgroups, schools and school parent committees, libraries etc are being expanded and strengthened;

- family literacy groups involving both adults and their children are running successfully, and a number of open learning centres is being piloted, along with literacy groups for migrant women, Travellers, and programmes for the unemployed in co-operation with the Community Employment Scheme;

- staff development programmes are underway on a modular inservice basis for tutors and literacy organisers;

- a quality framework for the adult literacy service has been developed and published by the National Adult Literacy Agency in collaboration with partners in Northern Ireland, Spain and UK;

- literacy programmes over the radio have been successfully piloted and evaluated in Mayo and Tipperary. Arising for the success of this initiative, the Department of Education and Science has commissioned the development of a TV series in literacy awareness and tuition for adults. Work is under way in collaboration with RTÉ and NALA with a view to broadcasting in the autumn;

- an Inter-Departmental Group on Literacy for the Unemployed has been established to develop an integrated response to addressing the literacy needs of the unemployed *"to jointly develop measures in consultation with the appropriate statutory agencies and expert groups, and report back to the Cabinet Committee on Social Inclusion, including estimated costs and available funding."*

4.4.3 Future Priorities in Adult Literacy Provision

Major elements of a National Adult Literacy Programme have already been put in place, and investment of £73.8m has been committed to this area in National Development Plan 2000-2006. Nonetheless, in view of:-

- the scale of the problem;

- the negative implications for the person's life chances;

- its intergenerational impact;

- the recognition that there is still a lot to learn in tackling the problem.

Future developments of a National Adult Literacy Programme will aim to:-

- continue to increase the number of clients reached, and the scale of investment – so that by the end of the Plan, an estimated 113,000 will have benefited from these services;

- prioritise those with lowest literacy levels;

- implement the quality framework which has been developed to monitor the effectiveness of the service;

- continue to develop new modes of targeting those affected, especially through the use of referral networks;

- provide for a greater orientation of education and training for the unemployed towards more basic levels of skill, including increased education and training content within the Community Employment Scheme, in order to bridge an important progression bridge to formal learning options for literacy students;

- encourage greater flexibility in enabling a combination and mixing of schemes so that FÁS, (The National Training & Employment Authority) and VECs can combine resources locally to best cater for emerging needs, e.g. CE participants could be referred to literacy training provided by education agencies, with the allowances paid by FÁS. Initiatives in this area have been successfully piloted, and FÁS is currently expanding such options to all regions;

- make optimum use of the Bridging Training Measures under the FÁS Action Plan for the Long-Term Unemployed which aim to support up to 1,500 long-term unemployed persons to advance onto mainstream training programmes. Literacy training is a key component of the bridging support;

- adopt NALA's Consortia Framework proposal as a basis for ensuring referral of those with literacy needs into appropriate training and education programmes as an integral part of the Employment Action Plan activation process;

- avail of the full range of complementary supports which can be made available by FÁS and the VECs in their overall programme. FÁS will continue to support the operation of programmes which provide back up to literacy schemes as a main part of their operation;

- develop new strategies to address the under-representation of men in literacy and other basic education programmes;

- explore the potential of ICT and broadcasting in literacy training;

- continue to develop specific initiatives for disadvantaged groups, i.e. people with disabilities, the homeless, Travellers, refugees and asylum seekers;

- expand provision for workplace literacy. The National Adult Literacy Agency has trained a number of tutors to provide literacy in the workplace and has promoted the availability of the service among employer organisations. A pilot has started in a large firm in the Dublin area, and similar initiatives are being planned for workers in the health and local authority sectors;

- increase collaboration with the public library service, based on the recommendations set out in the report of An Chomhairle Leabharlanna (The Library Council) entitled *The Right to Read - The Development of Partnership Strategies for the Promotion of Literacy in the Community; (1999)*

- increase collaboration with TEAGASC and other relevant interests in relation to meeting the literacy needs of farmers.

4.4.4 These developments will be accompanied by strategies to explore and address any remaining barriers to access to education and training generally due to anomalies in the social welfare and supplementary benefit system. In addition, the development of an educational adult guidance and counselling service will be crucial to the success of the National Adult Literacy programme.

4.4.5 Payment of Training Allowances/Welfare Payments

Reflecting the priority of Adult Literacy in Government Policy, it is intended that:-

- combinations of schemes will be used (literacy + CE, Literacy + Bridging) to optimum effect to enable participants on literacy programmes to be paid allowances;

- adult basic education and/or literacy programmes of duration of a minimum of 19.5 hours per week (as per CE) should be treated as full-time for the purpose of entitlement to a continued welfare payment.

- the Department of Social, Community and Family Affairs will examine the position of participants in approved part-time programmes insofar as it impacts on the requirements for persons in receipt of unemployment assistance/benefit to be available for full-time work. While it is envisaged that Deciding Officers would continue to have discretion in such matters, a key objective will be to provide the optimum opportunity for participants to improve their personal development, education, jobskills and literacy levels in order to be in a position to secure lasting employment;

- as a matter of policy, an integrated inter-Departmental approach will be adopted across all education and training and welfare programmes to the payment of allowances and the means-testing for secondary benefits, and that no changes are implemented without joint consultation with the range of Departments concerned.

In line with the Goodbody Report (1998), a Liaison Group has been set up to oversee policy and practice in relation to the retention of secondary benefits. There is a particular need to ensure equal treatment across the various schemes and the removal of anomalies and uncertainties which deter participation in education and training.

White Paper on Adult Education – Learning for Life

4.4.6 Literacy Within Schools

A major objective of the lifelong learning strategy set out in the *Programme for Prosperity and Fairness (2000)* is to provide a framework of supports which will facilitate the achievement of universal attainment of literacy and numeracy by the completion of primary education, and ensure the centrality of universal literacy and numeracy in all lifelong learning policy and practice. The most recent national survey of reading levels among primary pupils shows that there is still a high level of functional literacy problems among older primary pupils, and that up to one in ten of all fifth class pupils have difficulties in this area. This issue is being addressed through:-

- the expansion of the Home School Community Liaison and Remedial services under which all primary and post-primary schools now have access to a remedial service, and all designated schools in disadvantaged areas have a HSCL co-ordinator;

- the reform of the remedial service in line with the recommendations of an expert evaluation;

- the establishment of the National Educational Psychological Service and the legislation to raise the school-leaving age and establish an educational welfare board to monitor school attendance and support families at risk;

- the development of indicators at European level to compare achievement and work-relevant skills of 15-year olds;

- the provision of £6.5m grants to schools in 1999 for school library books on top of an earlier £5m scheme in 1998.

Under the *National Development Plan (1999)* an additional £11.75m is being provided for a co-ordinated early literacy measure to be put in place through a public awareness campaign, promotion of a National Reading Initiative, improvements in the effectiveness of school provision, the development of culturally appropriate supports including home/school/community co-operation, the development of support materials and systematic arrangements for the monitoring of pupil progress.

Research has shown the critical importance of practice both for children and adults, if literacy skills are to be developed and maintained. Reading to children, helping them develop their vocabulary and imagination and giving them encouragement will help ensure they become good readers. A child who goes home to a house which does not encourage reading or the development of reading skills is at risk of under-achieving at school irrespective of the quality of teaching. Experience within the adult literacy service has also demonstrated that adults can lose skills that they had on leaving school through disuse. A National Reading Initiative has been launched to raise public awareness of the importance of developing and promoting reading skills in classrooms, families and in the workforce, and enhancing literacy support skills among both formal and informal educators. The Initiative will run a number of national measures and act as a catalyst and support for local activities. These will include:-

- the re-focusing of literacy support schemes;

- an International Reading Conference;

- local seminars and workshops;

- parent support initiatives including baby book packs;

- paired/peer reading initiatives;

- reading at work promotions;

- vouchers, tokens and book discount schemes;

- promotion of the use of public libraries;

- book weeks/fortnights;

- teenage reading events;

- reading summer schools.

The Initiative will work closely with the adult literacy service, where family literacy programmes, involving parents and their children, are being expanded across the country.

4.4.7 Monitoring Impact

As stated, the challenge of addressing the adult literacy problem is now central to Government policy on Adult Education. Through the series of measures and greatly increased investment outlined in this Paper, the Government is confident that it can put in place a system that can make serious inroads into this major problem area.

In order to ensure that the National Adult Literacy Programme is realising its objectives, a National Adult Literacy Survey will be conducted three years hence, and at regular intervals thereafter. While it is desirable that this be conducted as part of an international comparative study akin to the seminal study of the OECD, in the absence of such an international study, a national study will be conducted.

4.5 Back to Education Initiative (BTEI)

4.5.1 The Back to Education Initiative is the second pillar of the Government's comprehensive strategy for Second Chance and Further Education outlined in this Paper. It will provide opportunities to return to learning for adults and provide a re-entry route for those in the workplace who wish to upgrade their skills in line with emerging needs. Access to information and communications technology training, electronic technician training, language skills, enterprise development, business, tourism, art and craft, childcare, and a broad range of disciplines within the industry and services sector will form part of the approach as will access to the Junior and Leaving Certificate examinations and other access programmes. A particular priority will be to increase provision at Foundation and Level 1 or equivalent for those with low skills, and to ensure a progression bridge is in place for students from the adult literacy service.

In recognition of the need to ensure systematic participation and benefit of those most affected by prolonged periods of unemployment, a study has been commissioned by the Department of Education and Science to identify and report on the outreach, recruitment, delivery and support strategies which are most effective in catering for those most in need.

The draft report highlights the three major influences on participation among those hardest to reach as:-

- a financial incentive to participate;

- a job guarantee or clear evidence of improved job prospects resulting from participation;

- the availability of suitable courses.

The recommendations focus on a re-balancing of policies towards transition to learning, a concerted effort to incentivise educational programmes, a re-focusing of programmes towards basic education levels, with greater flexibility, improved outreach, the capacity to offer one to one professional guidance, and more co-operation with other statutory and voluntary agencies.

4.5.2 In addition, the learning from a range of projects under HORIZON, YOUTHSTART, INTEGRA, NOW, the Women's Education Initiative, and the work of the Community Education sector also demonstrate the need for:-

- intensive outreach work in partnership with relevant community interests;

- localised provision within the community;

- a participative process and a key attention to dialogue, devoting time and resources to identifying needs, and demonstrating a willingness to adapt programmes to ensure relevance on an ongoing basis;

- flexible delivery and assessment arrangements;

- the removal of financial and cultural barriers;

- provision of intensive supports in the form of mentoring, advocacy, guidance, information and counselling;

- childcare and transport.

4.5.3 The overall target will be to increase the opportunities for participation in lifelong learning through a significant expansion of part-time options so that by the end of 2006 approximately 52,000 early school leavers and adults will be participating annually in further education, compared with a base figure at present of 32,000 i.e the initiative provides for expansion on a phased basis to enable up to 20,000 additional part-time places to be provided annually by the end of the Plan period. Within the National Development Plan, a sum of £1.027bn has been earmarked for the programme to cater for existing and expansion needs. Of this, at least £200m will be additional to the current base. It was not feasible within the timeframe of this White Paper to set out specific year to year targets for the initiative, as discussions on this issue, and on the industrial relations issues which impact on increased flexibility have still to be concluded with teacher and management interests and the Department of Finance. Overall, over the period 2000-2006, the target is that more than 320,000 participants will benefit from the measure.

4.5.4 Entry Points

The BTEI will provide for entry at a number of levels:-

- access to NCVA Foundation Level or Junior Certificate or equivalent levels of basic education for those who have no prior educational qualifications. A key priority at this level is to provide an effective bridge to certified learning for those progressing from the literacy service;

- access to NCVA Level 1 or Leaving Certificate or equivalent options for those who enter having completed lower second-level education;

- access to NCVA Level 2 or 3 programmes for those who have completed upper second-level education or are in a position to successfully complete a programme at this level. Within this area, key priorities will be the provision of ICT, electronic, engineering and e-commerce training, the development of foreign language proficiency, and the provision of childcare training.

4.5.5 In order to address needs in this area, the Back to Education Initiative will provide for an improvement in the pupil teacher ratio to 10:1 for all participants accessing the programme with less than upper second-level education. This will be conditional on providers

- demonstrating their promotion and recruitment strategies and the process of learner engagement through which needs were identified;

- demonstrating their linkages with relevant actors in the community at local level in regard to recruitment, referral and progression, and ensuring specific timetabling arrangements for outreach work;

- providing for access to national certification - this will be a pre-requisite for providers, although not compulsory for participants;

- complying with Departmental and Local Adult Learning Board co-ordination, reporting, accounting and management information procedures;

- ensuring learner participation in annual monitoring and evaluation strategies.

4.5.6 Four general categories of participant will be provided for:-

1. *Youthreach/Traveller/VTOS eligible on full-time courses* - For full-time participants, there will be free tuition plus a training allowance or social welfare payment.

2. *Other means-tested welfare or unemployment payment or Family Income Supplement recipient and their dependants and VTOS/ Youthreach eligible participants on part-time courses* - free tuition, will be provided, but entitlement to continued welfare payments will be subject to their satisfying the Department of Social, Community and Family Affairs regarding the conditions of the relevant scheme (for instance, in the case of unemployment payments, that the persons concerned are still available for and actively seeking work and that the course is likely to enhance their chances of gaining a job).

   For Youthreach/ Traveller participants on part-time courses who may not have an underlying welfare entitlement, there will be free tuition and a pro-rata training allowance may be payable, to be funded by the Department of Education and Science.

3. *Other unwaged participants with less than upper secondary education* (including pensioners with non-means tested pensions and those not in the labour force), who are not covered by categories 1 and 2 above - a reduction of fees will apply to a level of 30% of tuition costs.

4. *Remainder* - fees will be charged.

4.5.7 For the purposes of the scheme

Youthreach eligible = Young people who have left school early with either no qualifications or less than 5 Ds at junior cycle level. **Barriers to participation of this group in the 18-20 age group will be removed.** For Traveller there is no upper age limit, in order to encourage more parents to take part in the programme. Any payments due to Youthreach and Traveller participants will be funded by the Department of Education and Science in the form of a training allowance in lieu of social welfare entitlements.

VTOS eligible = Adults who are registered unemployed or signing for credits for at least six months and who are aged 21 or over. Dependent spouses, lone parents, and participants with disabilities who satisfy these criteria will also be eligible. Over time, and providing for the necessary transfer of resources, it is intended that overall responsibility for the payment of all existing training/ welfare

White Paper on Adult Education – Learning for Life

allowances for VTOS should transfer to the Department of Social, Community and Family Affairs, enabling the education sector to concentrate on its core functions.

Entitlement to a continued welfare payment or training allowance for VTOS/Youthreach eligible participants will apply only where full-time courses are attended. Where part-time attendance occurs, the continuation of the relevant welfare payment will be subject to the discretion of the Department of Social, Community and Family Affairs. In exercising such discretion, specific guidelines will be drawn up by the Department of Social, Community and Family Affairs in consultation with the Department of Education and Science to ensure a consistent and supportive strategy for those most in need.

4.5.8 Under Category 2 above, free tuition will apply to persons not in Category 1 who are:-

- in receipt of the welfare or health board payments set out at* below, and their dependents;

- medical card holders and their dependants; and

- recipients of the Family Income Supplement or their dependants.

*The social welfare and health board benefits to be covered by this arrangement will include:-

> Medical Card
>
> Supplementary Welfare Allowance
>
> Unemployment Benefit
>
> Unemployment Assistance
>
> Family Income Supplement
>
> Carer's Allowance
>
> One-Parent Family Payment
>
> Back-to-Work Allowance
>
> Community Employment
>
> Part-time Job Incentive Scheme
>
>
> Widow's and Widower's Non-Contributory Pension
>
> Blind Persons's Pension

Wicklow County Council
County Library Services

Pre-retirement allowance

Old Age Non-Contributory Pension

Orphan's Non-Contributory Pension

Disability Benefit, where this has been held for a continuous period of at least 6 months

Invalidity Pension

Disability Allowance.

4.5.9 It should be noted that many of the beneficiaries listed under Category 2 will continue to receive payments from the Department of Social, Community and Family Affairs. However, their continued payment will be discretionary, and subject to their satisfying the Department of Social, Community and Family Affairs as to their continued eligibility for the particular scheme (for instance, in the case of unemployment payments, that the persons concerned are still available for and actively seeking work, and that the course is likely to improve their chances of gaining a job.)

4.5.10 The Back to Education Initiative provides for a merging and continuation of existing levels of provision under Youthreach, Traveller, Vocational Training Opportunity Scheme (VTOS) and Post-Leaving Certificate courses, allied with a significant expansion of part-time options. It is important to note that what is envisaged is simply not "more of the same" although many of the existing programmes are highly successful in catering for their participant's needs, but rather the use of this framework to provide more flexible provision to cater for diverse needs.

Given the concerns expressed in the consultation process on the issue of fees, the implementation of the Back to Education Initiative will be monitored carefully to assess the impact of fees on the participation of different target groups, with a particular focus on those with less than upper second level education.

4.6 Learning Opportunities through ICT

4.6.1 In the Report of the Advisory Committee on Telecommunications it was noted that the forces of technology, competition and privatisation have led to a revolutionary transformation in the telecommunications and information service industries. Infrastructure competition (among fibre optic, cable, satellite and cellular networks) has resulted in exponential growth in communications capacity in both developing and industrialised nations. Rapid technological advances in digitalisation and semi-conductors have spawned vast industries, applications and opportunities for new entrepreneurs and established multinationals alike. Policies and practices which foster market-driven infrastructure and services are creating

White Paper on Adult Education – Learning for Life

new choices for people to live, work, learn and create. Most dramatic has been the advance of the Internet, which is quickly becoming the principal infrastructure for global electronic communications. There are many millions of users worldwide. It is estimated that by the end of the year 2000, the Internet alone will create a single global network of over 300 million users. It will be the fastest growing network ever in the history of communications. More and more, the Internet will be used as a means of conducting consumer and business transactions (e-Commerce).

The growth of the ICTs inevitably means that increasing numbers of adults will look to access education and training opportunities through ICT. Educational institutions in Ireland, while to the forefront in teaching about ICT, have been slow in utilising ICT in their teaching, particularly in the development of out of classroom teaching. While this has general implications for the education sector in the context of global competition, it also reduces the range and choice of possibilities which adult learners in Ireland can avail of in their learning pursuits.

Advances in the development and applications of new technologies pose both a challenge and an opportunity for adult learners. As a challenge, literacy in the new technologies is an increasingly essential requirement for participation in daily life. An ever-increasing number of everyday functions are being undertaken electronically together with an ever-increasing range of opportunities which require computer literacy.

As an opportunity for adult learners, ICT provides a whole new mechanism for overcoming distance; for accessing information from one's home or workplace; for pursuing accredited learning programmes as more and more institutions adapt their programmes for electronic delivery and for interaction with other learners in a virtual classroom environment. While recognising the limitations of ICT in educational applications and conceding that it is better to look to the virtual learning environment to supplement rather than replace the actual one, it is nonetheless contended that the application of ICT in Adult Education practice in Ireland is as yet only in its infancy and a vast potential remains to be tapped. If this potential is to be tapped, and indeed if Ireland as a society is to maintain its position vis-à-vis other countries in the information revolution, it is imperative that the learning blocks in accessing ICT are removed.

4.6.2 There are compelling reasons for integrating ICTs into the education and training systems. Firstly, there are vocational and economic reasons for promoting the use of ICTs in education. Knowledge and familiarity with new technologies will be an important dimension of employability in the information society. This is of particular relevance to Ireland in light of the increasing demand for these skills and their importance for the continued growth of the Irish economy.

Secondly, there are pedagogic reasons for adopting new technologies in classrooms. ICTs can improve the quality of the educational experience by providing rich, exciting and motivating environments for learning. Most educational researchers refer to the high motivation evidenced in students using ICTs for learning. Others refer to the opportunities which ICTs present to encourage the development of creativity, imagination and self-expression. The use of computers can accelerate positive trends such as increased emphasis on information handling and problem-solving and reduced emphasis on memorising facts. ICTs can make colleges become more collaborative environments for both students and tutors. Indeed this collaboration can extend beyond college boundaries to include co-operation for learning at a distance both within and between colleges, businesses and countries.

Thirdly, there are social benefits. It is clearly important that all people, regardless of social or economic background, should have equal access to new technologies. A range of reports has pointed out the danger of the creation of a two-tier society of information haves and have-nots. The Green Paper and the data presented above provide convincing evidence of the relative levels of educational disadvantage experienced by Irish adults as they get older, when compared with younger age groups. It is likely that such comparative disadvantage is not only replicated in the ICT area but that the gaps between older and younger age groups are even wider in this area.

4.6.3 The Government's *Action Plan on Implementing the Information Society in Ireland (1999)* sets out a strategy to promote eBusiness, eOrganisations and eGovernment, to foster affordable and inclusive ICT infrastructure and services, and to encourage participation by those who are currently excluded. In addition, the strategy to address skill needs in the computer software and technician areas, the new Accelerated Technician Programme and the IT industry led FastTrack IT Initiative mentioned in Chapter 6 all play an important role in contributing to the development of the Information Society.

4.6.4 Recognising the growing importance of computer literacy for adults generally the Government will provide for a **National Adult Basic ICT Skills Programme** as part of the Back to Education Initiative.

The main elements of this programme will include:-

- a national programme of ICT training up to and including NCVA Level Two standard, to cater for the 4 categories of student outlined above;

- technical support for adult education providers to enable them to maintain, upgrade and network their ICT facilities;

- appropriate support to ensure that where premises are used outside school hours for adult education programmes, the ICT facilities will be re-set at the end of class to make sure that they are available for ready use for the daytime work of the school;

- complementary staff development and curriculum support arrangements.

This programme will be the first national campaign in IT training for Irish adults.

It is considered by Government as an essential element of a national infrastructure for Adult Education in that it will provide the basic tools for ongoing learning through ICTs.

In addition to learning about ICT, the Government is also concerned that Irish adults are enabled to access new learning opportunities via ICT. With an ever-increasing internet usage in Ireland and anticipated technological innovations, the potential of this tool to facilitate mass education participation is evident. Particular priorities using technology as a medium will be training in the IT area itself, literacy, language training and the development of a global civil society.

4.7 Broadcasting

Digital televisual broadcasting, to be introduced by RTE in 2001 will provide for a designated education channel. Broadcasting has traditionally played an important if small role in Irish adult education. The onset of a designated television channel for education purposes opens up a new era for broadcasting in education and will provide a multiplicity of opportunities to providers to work collaboratively with RTE in developing an Educational Television service.

An evaluation of a Literacy Through the Airwaves local radio initiative developed by the National Adult Literacy Agency and Tipp FM, and Castlebar Community Radio and Co Mayo VEC concluded that:

> "Radio is a potentially powerful resource, both in assisting literacy learners to access help and improve their skills, and in providing a learning resource for learners, tutors and literacy schemes in maximising the possibilities which the ongoing expansion of the literacy sector is currently undergoing". (p.44, 1999)

This pilot project, funded by the Department of Education and Science and by the Independent Radio and Television Commission, not only demonstrated the potential application of radio to literacy provision, but also showed how collaborative processes between a stakeholder - NALA - and a "carrier" could be developed with the emergence of a designated broadcasting channel. Clearly there will be an ever greater requirement for such collaborative arrangements.

It is unlikely that many of the Adult Education providers in Ireland could meet the expensive front-loading requirements of TV production or even of adapting existing or new courses for broadcasting purposes. The National Adult Learning Council in association with the Department of Public Enterprise and the RTE Authority will establish a Task Force on Broadcasting and Education to assess the resource implications of a comprehensive educational broadcasting service and to identify possible sources of such resources. The Task Force will also be asked to make recommendations on a strategy to ensure the supply of a cadre of educationalists with the skills necessary to work with broadcasting professionsl in translating educational materials into suitable formats for broadcasting. A key goal will be to expand learning options to a mass audience in such areas as ICT, language, literacy, and parenting.

Programme production and the preparation of course materials are of course just some of the ways in which providers can become involved in educational broadcasting. It would be critically important also to provide for avenues for certified learning options through broadcast media in collaboration with educational providers. Accreditation of such courses within emerging developments under the National Qualifications Framework would also significantly boost the development of this exciting area.

Generally, if educational broadcasting is to become a reality in Ireland and is to play its full part in lifelong learning provision in the country, it will require an active involvement of all the main education players In every sector - from pre-school onwards. It is important that this project adopts a learner-centred approach which will raise new challenges to educationalists and broadcasters as they combine their expertise in this most exciting new departure.

4.8 Self-funded part-time Adult Education

4.8.1 The role of schools.

Second-level schools have been at the core of provision of Adult Education in Ireland. The Vocational Education Act (1930) assigned the task of developing a suitable system of "continuation education" to the VECs, a task which was taken up by the vocational schools throughout the country.

In more recent years the community and comprehensive sector has emerged as a major provider of night classes and daytime education opportunities for adults. The contribution of this sector in this area is all the more noteworthy considering the institutional disincentive with which it worked up to the publication of the Green Paper, whereby 'night school' points leading to the creation of an additional posts of responsibility in the school had resulted in a loss to the 'day school' teaching provision. Despite this constraint, the sector has made a contribution which greatly exceeds what might be expected in terms of its size in the overall second-level sector.

In recent years the Department of Education and Science in association with the ASTI and the JMB have undertaken a pilot programme in Adult Education in the voluntary secondary sector. A recent evaluation of this project showed how a

> *"relatively small investment (had) yielded major returns in terms of course provision, numbers of participants, engaging schools in the process and in building relationships between the schools, parents*

and wider communities in which they are located". (p.34, 1999)

The evaluation went on to show that the schools valued the programmes primarily for their contribution to the core second-level objectives of the school in that, in building relationships with parents and other community interests, the school was better positioned to meet its objectives with its core group of 12-18 year olds.

Department of Education and Science figures show that in 1998/99 almost 89,800 adult students participated in self-financed part-time education in VEC schools, and nearly 50,600 participants took such classes in the community and comprehensive schools sector. These figures call attention to the major role that the second-level schools have played in the Adult Education sector, in addition to their more traditional second-level function. As with trends the previous year, 73% of participants on these programmes were women.

Falling numbers in the 12-18 year age cohort have enabled many second-level schools to look at providing further education opportunities for constituencies other than the conventional second-level student. The most noteworthy development here has been the growth of the Post-Leaving Certificate (PLC) sector referred to above, where student numbers have doubled to 24,337 over the past 10 years. These courses have in the past decade come to provide an important progression route for about 14% of all school leavers each year, in addition to becoming an important re-entry route for adults returning to learning. 34% of PLC students are aged 21 or over.

Second-level schools, as stated, have tended to see their involvement in Adult Education as one of providing night classes or, in some cases, daytime education opportunities for a discrete adult or further education population, quite separate from that of its mainstream 12-18 year old population. It is envisaged that the second-level schools will continue to play this role. The challenge of a lifelong learning focus, however, is of a more profound structural and organisational nature. The adoption of such a focus would seek for far closer integration and mutuality between two previously discrete sectors, with much greater intergenerational mix, not just in day provision but in night provision also. This, however, is part of a long-term debate. In the immediate term, the Government recognises the adult learning infrastructure which the countrywide networks of second-level schools and teachers provide and which, if adequately and appropriately resourced, has a major role to play in enhancing the learning opportunities of the adult population.

4.8.2 Arrangements for Night-Time, Part-Time Self-Funded Adult Education

Recognising this potential the Government has decided:-

- to abolish the self-financing principle for *certain categories of student*. Up to now, schools which offered part-time Adult Education classes were obliged to fund all aspects of the provision from fees. This will be of particular benefit to rural schools where small populations meant that the self-financing requirement was extremely difficult to meet. Students to whom such arrangements apply will be designated as Back to Education Initiative students, and may either participate in stand-alone BTEI courses, or dispersed in night-time predominantly self-funded classes;

- to expand the existing pilot start-up ASTI/JMB scheme to the Community and Comprehensive and VEC sectors so that it applies on a rolling, once-off basis to all schools in an Adult Education start-up situation. Schools in all sectors who have not previously been involved in adult education provision may apply for a £5,000 grant on a once off basis. The grant is designed as a catalyst to facilitate the first stages of involvement in provision, and may be used for equipment and materials, staff development, preparing accommodation, advertising, administration and waiver of student fees in hardship cases. The size of the fund will be increased from £100,000 per annum to £160,000 per annum to enable new centres to be accommodated on a phased basis. The scheme will end at the end of 2006 when the National Development Plan has been completed. The scheme is at present administered by the ASTI/JMB and the structure will be widened to include the other interest;

- to allocate additional teaching hours where necessary to compensate day schools for posts of responsibility awarded in respect of night students;

- to promote a local participant fee structure designed to cover all costs other than posts of responsibility i.e at least 130% of tuition costs should be recovered in fees in order to provide for tuition, premises, equipment and materials overheads, the recruitment of secretarial, technical and care-taking support, advertising and technical support. Unwaged students with less than upper secondary education engaging in second-chance courses who do not otherwise have an underlying entitlement to the Back to Education Initiative may have a reduction to 30% of tuition costs. In the case of designated BTEI students, the fees would be borne by the Department;

- to make arrangements for payment of an additional allowance to principals providing a part-time, mainly self-funded Adult Education programme. The costs of this are to be borne by the Department;

- to provide for the designation of a post of a Director of Adult Education in each school offering a part-time mainly self-funded programme of at least 1,500 enrolment hours. The level of allowances, the appointment of additional Assistant Directors and Special Duties posts, allied with reductions in teaching hours will apply progressively as the size of the Adult Education programme increases. The costs of all such allowances will be borne by the Department;

- to enable schools and VECs to retain any surplus fee income remaining after operational costs are met for re-investment in Adult Education. This will require further consultation with management interests to ensure transparent and appropriate accounting and tracking arrangements for expenditure in this area;

- to ensure that Directors of Adult Education appointed in all schools co-ordinate their activities and maintain close contact with the Adult Education Organiser in the area and all other relevant agencies so as to ensure a co-ordinated, area-based approach. Compliance with the reporting requirements of the Department, those of the present Adult Education Boards, and emerging developments under the proposed Local Adult Learning Boards will be a key part of this process.

This approach is designed to focus on part-time mainly self-funded Adult Education provision including personal and social development, hobby and leisure courses of an academic or practical nature and second chance courses. It will also provide some opportunities for increased activity in the sphere of parental education and support on a community wide basis. In that context, links with the Home School Community Liaison service and with the first and second-level sectors will be a crucial part of the approach.

As stated earlier, 1.1m adults aged 15-64, or 44.8% of the population in this age group in Ireland, have less than upper second-level education. Of these, 529,600 have not attained lower secondary education. Some 61.5% of all unemployed people have less than upper second-level education. Clearly, notwithstanding the feedback in the consultation process which followed the Green Paper, a strategy which would allow guaranteed free access for all of this group in returning to learning is unaffordable at this stage. It would risk involving a significant displacement investment in relation to the 140,000+ adults who are currently engaging in self-funded programmes in the sector, and would divert much needed investment from the development of core supports such as guidance, counselling and childcare, and from investment to improve and expand the flexibility and relevance of provision. Nonetheless, through the measures proposed in this White Paper, the self-funded component of Further Education will be significantly enhanced. This will ensure that it continues to expand and diversify its provision in line with emerging need.

4.9. Capital

Recognising the validity of the concerns raised in the consultation process, the Government will provide for a specific capital allocation for the Further Education sector. This will increase on a phased basis to a level of at least £10m per annum.

The funds will be used for:-

- building in areas where rental is not feasible and no other suitable premises are available;

- adaptation of premises to cater for students with disabilities and to comply with health and safety requirements;

- investment in ICT facilities, and ICT networks and upgrading of equipment;

- purchase, where necessary, of additional facilities for adult education use;

- development of stand-alone centres for adult education and multi-plexes, in line with local needs.

With regard to new school buildings in the second-level sector, all such building will be adult learning proofed, so as to ensure that they are suitable for use by adults in a variety of uses both within and outside of school hours. The insurance arrangements for schools will be reviewed to ensure adequate cover for after hours usage by other community interests, with the proviso that a care-taker must be funded by the group concerned as part of the arrangements.

In supporting arrangements under the Back to Education Initiative, the Department will provide pro-rata funding for:-

- tuition, equipment, materials and advertising costs;

- caretaking, heat and light and overheads for all premises used for the Initiative;

- technician support, especially in the area of maintenance of IT equipment and of other educational aids.

Where schools are being used for Adult Education on a self-funded basis, fees will also be set at a level to cover such costs. On this basis, in the context of a guarantee that all marginal extra expenses associated with Adult Education would be covered, that insurance cover would be adequate and IT facilities and premises left in good order for the following day, it is expected that there should be an increased availability of school premises generally for after hours Adult Education provision.

A review of compliance with educational needs, health and safety and disability access requirements will be conducted on a phased basis of all centres being used for Adult Education. The outcome of the review will inform priorities for investment under the capital fund.

In addition, where centres are currently rented, VECs and other providers will be asked to explore the feasibility of switching to a rental purchase agreement based on the same general level of annual outlay. Investment in refurbishment of rented premises by the State will be subject to a deed of trust being drawn up to ensure that, in the event of the premises no longer being available for educational reasons, the unexpired value of the State's investment will be repaid.

Each Local Adult Learning Board will be asked to compile a directory of premises which are suitable and available for adult and community education in their respective areas. In particular they will be asked to work with county libraries in more closely integrating their facilities, resources and expertise into the broader Adult Education provision of their area.

4.10 Review of PLC sector

The Post Leaving Certificate (PLC) Programme was introduced in 1985 to provide appropriate education and training for young people to bridge the gap between school and work. PLC's also provide an alternative route to higher education in the Institutes of Technology. The numbers of students participating on PLC courses has increased steadily over the past 10 years from over 12,000 students in 1989/90 to 24,337 in 1999/2000.

With the expansion of disciplines, the growth of large specialist centres, the introduction of national assessment and certification arrangements, quality upgrading, changing technology, and increased levels of resources devoted to advertising and recruitment, workplace linkages, progression and follow-up, there is an urgent need to re-assess the organisational, management and ancillary services needed to support the programme.

The Department will establish a Working Group with an independent chairperson representing management and practitioner interests to review needs in this area. The Group will examine and make recommendations as necessary regarding the organisational, support, development, technical and administrative structures and resources required in schools and colleges with large scale PLC provision having regard to good practice in related areas across the system and in other countries.

This review will play particular attention to schools and colleges where the number of PLC students exceeds 150, and will examine the structures needed in centres of varying size.

The review will make recommendations in relation to:-

(a) the appropriate physical infrastructure which should underpin provision in regard to meeting the quality demands and health and safety requirements of programmes;

(b) the level and structure of administrative, technical, management, teaching and guidance, student and ancillary supports which should apply in the PLC sector.

4.11 Conclusion

This White Paper marks a new departure in setting out a comprehensive framework of State-funded and self-funded programmes to address the low levels of educational attainment of Irish adults. This will provide for a continuum of Further and Second-chance Education to be put in place ranging from literacy and basic education skills to Post Leaving Certificate level. The National Adult Literacy Programme and the Back to Education Initiative incorporate a range of allowances, incentives and flexible delivery modes which will target the key priority groups of those with low levels of literacy, those with incomplete second-level education and other specific disadvantaged groups. The impact of these programmes will be monitored and assessed on an on-going basis so as to ensure that they meet their targets.

In significantly improving flexibility and organisational structures for self-funded night-time programmes, the White Paper is both validating the contribution of this sector to date in Adult Education and looking forward with optimism to a greatly expanded and re-invigorated role for the sector in the future. In launching the first National Programme in ICT training for adults, the Paper is addressing one of the major knowledge barriers which adults increasingly face both in a work and education context. Equally, the capital expenditure measures enunciated will not only enhance provision for adults in a direct way, but will also serve to focus the attention of policy makers and providers throughout education on the adult learner.

Chapter 5
Community
Education

CHAPTER 5
Community Education

5.1 The growth, significance and innovation of the Community Education movement were highlighted in the Green Paper (1998). Its contribution was particularly acknowledged in the following areas:-

- in reaching large numbers of participants, frequently in disadvantaged settings;

- in pioneering new approaches to teaching and learning in non-hierarchical, community-based settings

- in taking the lived experience of the participants as a starting point.

It was also noted in the Green Paper that the concept of Community Education is subject to a variety of definitions and perceptions. On the one hand, it has been seen as an extension of the service provided by second and third-level education institutions into the wider community. In this sense, it could be seen to incorporate almost all adult learning opportunities provided by the formal education sectors at community level - it is education in the community but not of the community.

5.2 A second view of Community Education - and the one that was adopted in the Green Paper - sees it in a more ideological sense as a process of communal education towards empowerment, both at an individual and a collective level. Such an approach to Community Education sees it as an interactive challenging process, not only in terms of its content but also in terms of its methodologies and decision-making processes.

During the consultation on the Green Paper a number of commentators sought to clarify the distinction between Community Development and Community Education. If one sees Community Development as a process in which those who are affected by decisions are empowered to participate in making decisions, it is apparent that the distinction between it and this second type of Community Education is at least blurred. They share a common goal of the collective empowerment of the participants based on an analysis of the structural barriers to people's life chances, although Community Development usually implies a dimension of organised action or activism following such an analysis.

5.3 Community-Based Women's Groups

Community Education has evolved in Ireland in recent years as an ideologically driven, highly innovative and large-scale Adult Education provision consisting mainly of self-directed women's groups. These groups have been central in the defining character of Community Education in Ireland and merit particular recognition for their contribution to date.

Such groups began to emerge in the early 1980s in Ireland, mostly in urban working-class areas, badly affected by high rates of unemployment and dealing with high levels of youth dependency.

5.4 Community Education : A Feminist Critique

According to Smyth, feminist education is *"where women decide what they need to know and how they want to use that knowledge"*. It embodies:-

- an openness to alternative structures and a critique of existing ones;

- an emphasis on sharing in learning rather than competing in it;

- a blurring of distinctions between the 'teacher' and the 'taught';

- an endeavour to locate personal, individual experiences within the broader social and political context;

- the elimination of hierarchy;

- an orientation to enhanced educational and vocational progression for the participants;

- a challenge to the dominant modes of assessment and accreditation.

Perhaps the most fundamental point regarding the conjuncture of feminist education with community-based women's education is the common starting point being the lived experience of the women participants. In starting from that point, as opposed to a syllabus or institution-driven agenda, Community Education assumes a different character to all other forms of formal education, not merely in terms of its content but in terms of the relationships between the participants themselves; between the participants and tutors; the learning process and outcomes and the modes of assessment.

Similarly, a recent report of the Women's Education Research and Resource Centre in UCD (1999) on such groups talked about an

> *"approach to learning based on active involvement, inclusive contribution, and developmental participation for adult women... (as) one which potentially redefines education and unfolds what has traditionally been a well wrapped, highly reverential male domain"* (p.26).

In starting with the reality of the women's own lives, such education is not only modelling feminist principles but demonstrating a core principle of all Adult Education activity with marginalised groups. Such a starting point also enables the learner to identify the forces shaping one's own life and to move towards changing one's own situation - a process of moving from the personal to the political.

In many instances where such groups developed, they did so with the active support of the local Adult Education Organiser and also the occasional support of other agencies, particularly AONTAS and the National Women's Council in Ireland. Generally, however, they received little financial support or recognition from the formal education system and have been primarily funded through the Department of Social, Community and Family Affairs, EU Community Initiatives, particularly NOW, HORIZON, YOUTHSTART, and INTEGRA, and through the Local Urban and Rural Development Programme.

The EU Community Initiatives were important not only in providing a major boost to the ongoing development of these groups, but also in ensuring systematic technical support and evaluation to their activities. In 1998, recognising the value and the potential of the sector, the Department of Education and Science launched the Women's Education Initiative.

Alongside community-based women's groups, the Community Education movement has also flourished in a range of other disadvantaged contexts. The community development programme of the Deptartment of Social, Community and Family Affairs was launched in 1989 and now works in nearly one hundred disadvantaged communities, both urban and rural, throughout the country. Similarly, through the work of the Area-Based Partnerships, Community Education has focused on issues of inclusion as they affect marginalised groups such as Travellers, people with disabilities, rural smallholders and the elderly.

5.5 Support to the Development of Community Education

The community-based sector is amongst the most dynamic, creative and relevant components of Adult Education provision in Ireland. The increasing importance of the community and voluntary sector generally in influencing policies and services to address marginalisation is highlighted in the National Anti-Poverty Strategy, in the stress on a widening of consultation mechanisms under the Public Sector Strategic Management Initiative, in the participation of the sector on the National

Economic and Social Forum and on EU monitoring committees, and in the major role played by the sector in recent National Partnership Agreements.

Key characteristics of the community education sector are:-

- its non-statutory nature;

- its rootedness in the community, not just in terms of physical location, but also in that its activists have lived and worked for many years within the community, have a deep knowledge and respect for its values, culture, and circumstances, and an understanding of community needs and capacity;

- its problem-solving flexible focus based on trust;

- its process rather than syllabus focus - participants are engaged from the outset as equal partners in identifying needs, designing and implementing programmes, and adapting them on an ongoing basis;

- its respect for participants and its reflection of their lived experience;

- its concern with communal values and its commitment to match curriculum and pedagogy with the needs and interests of students;

- its promotion of personalised learning and flexibility within the environment of a learning group. Its goals include not just individual development but also collective community advancement, especially in marginalised communities;

- its placing a key emphasis on providing the supports necessary for successful access and learning – particularly guidance, mentoring, continuous feedback and dialogue, childcare etc;

- its collective social purpose and inherently political agenda - to promote critical reflection, challenge existing structures, and promote empowerment, improvement so that participants are enabled to influence the social contexts in which they live;

- its promotion of participative democracy. It sees a key role for Adult Education in transforming society.

The Government is committed to providing the Community Education sector with the recognition and the resources that reflect its importance and which can release further potential. In supporting the sector the Government is also concerned that its innovation and responsiveness are preserved despite the formalisation of systems which Government support implies.

5.6 Community Education Facilitators

It is proposed to appoint a national team of 35 Community Education Facilitators to be based in the Local Adult Boards with responsibility for:-

- promoting the development and nurturing of new community based learning groups;

- providing support to new and existing Community Education groups in the form of technical, administrative and educational inputs;

- developing and encouraging partnerships and links with statutory and other providers;

- promoting the role of the sector in supporting outreach and referral to the statutory sector;

- liaising on accreditation and certification issues;

- helping community education interests to access funding;

- networking of groups, both nationally and locally, supporting their participation in community fora, and facilitating a co-ordinated input from the sector into the work of Local Adult Learning Boards and the County/City Development Boards;

- sharing good practice from the sector and supporting the mainstreaming of relevant lessons into national policy and practice;

- reporting to the Local Adult Learning Boards on developments and provision, and informing the work of the National Adult Learning Council.

White Paper on Adult Education – Learning for Life

The Community Education Facilitators will be required to demonstrate a deep-rooted knowledge of the communities they serve and a clear understanding and empathy with the philosophy and processes of community education.

5.7 Technical Support

The National Adult Learning Council will be asked to establish a specific unit to co-ordinate, assist and monitor the work of the Community Education facilitators. This unit will bring the collective expertise of the many statutory and non-statutory support bodies active in this area to bear on the work and priorities of the Facilitators. The unit, together with the team of local Community Education Facilitators will therefore work closely with a number of agencies to provide technical support to the following sectors:-

- community based women's groups

- men's groups

- Travellers and other ethnic minorities

- people with disabilities

- community arts groups

- older people

The Community Education Technical Support Unit will be the pivotal link between the National Adult Learning Council and the Community Education sector. While it is not envisaged that it will play a direct funding role with community groups it will support their capacity building and the development of innovative practices from within a Community Education model. It will also engage in or commission research in the field, and provide for the work of the sector to be evaluated systematically. This work will also focus on the extent to which community education participants are successful in accessing mainstream education and training, and make recommendations on how such progression can be further enhanced. The National Adult Learning Council will work closely with the National Qualifications Authority of Ireland to facilitate the co-ordinated development of flexible and relevant accreditation and certification arrangements for the sector.

5.8 Resourcing Community Groups

As part of the consultation in preparing the White Paper, community-based groups drew attention not only to the inadequacy of the financial and other resources at their disposal, but also to the short-term nature of much of their funding; the multiplicity of funding sources; the differing demands of the respective funders and the fact that many of these groups were the indirect beneficiaries of funding allocated to other bodies rather than allocated directly to the groups themselves.

Recognising the empowerment objectives of these groups, the Government is concerned to provide:-

(a) a more streamlined funding mechanism;

(b) long-term funding;

(c) a separate budget line for Community Education in the non-statutory sector, to be funded in the longer term locally through the Local Adult Learning Boards.

5.9 To achieve this, **10% of the annual increase provided under the Back to Education Initiative will be allocated on an ongoing basis exclusively for the development of Community Education**. Over the period to 2006 this will ensure at least £20m extra investment by the Department of Education and Science in the sector, in addition to the base provision of £1m annually which is already given to VECs under the Adult Literacy and Community Education Scheme. This investment will be complemented by continued outlay under initiatives operated by the Department of Social, Community and Family Affairs and the local development initiatives of the Area-Based Partnerships. It is intended that the funds will be allocated initially either through the Department of Education and Science and the National Adult Learning Council when it is established, but that when the size of the overall fund grows to a sufficient level, it will be allocated through the Ladult Learning Boards, which will be in a better position to assess local need.

Community Education providers will access funds through a competitive bidding process on the basis of a national scheme. Criteria for the scheme, implementation and reporting arrangements and performance indicators will be drawn up nationally in consultation with appropriate national interest groups from the statutory and community and voluntary sectors. In that context, a key requirement will be that projects selected for funding demonstrate the characteristics that have been identified as being particular to the sector. The funds will not exceed the unit cost norms available to the statutory sector for the client groups involved. However, an important focus of the initiative will be to overcome the barriers regarding premises and support services that have been highlighted in the consultation process. It is envisaged that funds will be allocated on the basis of 3-year programmes of activity.

Such funding will provide a major resource base to these groups in their ongoing programming and in their longer-term development. By providing direct funding support to these groups, the Government is giving tangible recognition to them for the work they do, not only with their members but also recognising that they can play a useful role in providing other educational and training inputs into the community.

5.10 In addition, under the equality measures in the *2000-2006 National Development Plan, 1999* the Women's Education Initiative, which was established in 1998 to assist projects to address the current gaps in provision for educationally disadvantaged women, has been expanded and widened as the Education Equality Initiative, to cater also for the needs of educationally disadvantaged men. Funding of £3.5m has been provided for this Initiative over the period of the Plan. The aim of the projects selected under this initiative will be to address gaps in the provision of education and training for specific marginalised groups, to carry out outreach and pre-development work, to facilitate progression of groups and individuals, to promote learning partnerships and to mainstream learning, to share good practice and to inform policy.

5.11 Community Groups as Providers

There are in the region of 1,000 daytime education women's groups throughout the country. While data on numbers participating in these groups are sketchy, AONTAS, the National Association for Adult Education, calculates that there are up to 30,000 women participating in groups affiliated to them. Evaluations of the Local Urban and Rural Development Programme have highlighted the work of the Partnerships in networking with over 3000 community and voluntary sector groups with a role or interest in social inclusion issues. Clearly, the level of funding available will require that criteria for a rigorous prioritisation process are developed, and that joint frameworks for accountability and quality assurance form an integral part of the approach. A balance must be struck between the need to support innovation and empowerment through local initiatives, particularly in disadvantaged areas, and the need for systematic and strategic investment in the development and expansion of core services within the statutory sector. The challenge will be to mainstream the learning from successful models within policy and practice to ensure the State sector programmes evolve flexibly in line with needs, while developing and promoting the role of community education as a sector in its own right, and as a policy voice, within overall Adult Education provision.

Apart from the inherent value of the work Community Education groups do, it is reasonable to assume that both in their person-centred, non-threatening methodologies and in their highly integrated connections into the local community, such groups already have the potential for education and training delivery into communities or groups which are frequently hard to reach by the formal providers. As investment increases overall in Adult Education and training, it is desirable that community education interests play an important role in the delivery of education and training, through linking with statutory agencies in a formalised outreach role. This would lead to a new synergy between the sectors, providing the greatest return from the community sector's capacity to innovate and engage with the most marginalised in society. Recognising this potential, the National Adult Learning Council will be asked to formulate a strategy for the ongoing promotion of community sector involvement in programme delivery, in consultation with the statutory providers and community education groups.

This does not imply a passive, delivery position for the community education sector – something that would be at variance with its core ideology. On the contrary, a generalised involvement of the sector in a collaborative process with statutory priorities would mean that the sector would become involved, not only in targeting or reaching the desired participants, but would also become involved in curriculum planning and design and in decisions regarding pedagogical approaches.

There is some concern amongst community-based women's groups that greater resources going into the sector could serve to create a cache of professional workers and could culminate in an ironic way in displacing the current body of activists in favour of paid professionals recruited through third-level training programmes. While it is desirable that the sector is enriched by as wide a range of contributors as possible, it is important that local activists who would wish to upgrade their skills and qualifications as community educators – whether they be women in the community or members of other excluded groups engaged in community education activity - have every opportunity to engage in ongoing training and the enhancement of their qualifications through third-level programmes tailored to their needs. The extent to which third-level institutions respond to this issue will be an important element of the assessment and resourcing of the strategic plans of these institutions, discussed elsewhere in this White Paper. Experience not only with community based women's education groups, but also with other excluded groups, particularly Travellers, has shown the benefits of upskilling members of a community to provide an educational programme into that community.

5.12 In summary, this White Paper envisages a key role for the community education sector:-

- as a provider in its own right which needs to be resourced;

- as an important voice, locally and nationally, in Adult Education and training policy development, innovation, and review;

- in engaging in partnerships with the statutory sector;

- as a key agent in successfully meeting the needs of communities and groups who are most marginalised.

5.13 Community Arts

Paralleling the growth of the Community Education sector in Ireland, there has been a rapid growth in Community Arts activity. Community Arts in the Irish Adult Education sector tends to combine concerns with the pursuit of art for its own sake with concerns to utilise the Arts in attaining other learning, particularly in the areas of personal development and social analysis.

Experience of such programmes as Youthreach has already demonstrated the importance as the Arts as a vocational area, its role in personal development and confidence building, in encouraging self-expression, team-work and inter-personal skills, and as a means of sensitively exploring issues of direct relevance to participants' daily lives. These include relationships, behaviour, strategies for handling conflict, coping skills and family, community or other presenting difficulties.

Whether as an end in themselves or as a means to an end, the Arts in general provide for an enriching personal and cultural life; extend the limits of individual endeavour and potential; enhance the quality of life in a society and provide for an holistic experience when employed as a vehicle for reflective learning. As a growing sector, the Arts also provide job opportunities in an increasing range of areas and both directly and indirectly enhance the economic capacity of the area. Reflecting and supporting this potential a number of Institutes of Technology, Universities, the National College of Art and Design, PLC programmes, and voluntary groups such as CAFÉ, have developed a number of programmes in the area of Community Arts.

The Arts Council is an autonomous statutory body appointed by the Government to provide and assist the Arts and to develop public awareness and appreciation of the Arts. In its recently published *Work Plan 1999-2002, (1999)* the Council has set three objectives:-

- to promote excellence and innovation in the Arts;

- to develop participation in and audiences for the Arts;

- to build capacity in the Arts sector.

Apart from the obvious educational implications of such an agenda, the Plan makes explicit reference to the field of Community Arts.

5.14 While not attempting to define Community Arts, the Plan notes the rapid growth of the phenomenon and the "widespread and eclectic" nature of its activity. It observes that *"where overall aims and objectives of Community Arts work are clear, well managed and resourced, and where artists of experience and skill have been engaged, participative artistic work of great potential and high quality has emerged over the life of the last Arts Plan" (p.50, 1999).*

An inherent tension between the demands of a quality art form and a quality participative process using an arts vehicle is recognisable in the literature and the debate around Community Arts. There may even be some tension between the desire to educate people in the Arts and that of educating people through the Arts. The Government is concerned to develop closer links between the Arts promotion agencies and Adult Education providers, especially at local level. At national level, this can be progressed building on the work of the existing inter-agency committee which includes the Department of Education and Science, the Department of Arts Heritage, Gaeltacht and the Islands, and the Arts Council. At local level, closer links will be encouraged between education providers and Local Authorities. It is anticipated that County Arts Officers will work closely with the Local Learning Boards.

5.15 Complementary Therapies

The growth of complementary therapies has been poorly documented in Ireland. It can be stated however, that there is wide public interest in such therapies, illustrated in the growth of the area in Adult Education provision in recent years and in the prominence of practitioners in this area in the Green Paper consultation process.

In some senses the growth path of these therapies mirrors that of Adult and Community Education, apart altogether from the fact that they frequently share common principles. The complementary therapies, like many aspects of Adult Education, have grown up outside of the formal system. The sector provides a critique of the medical model, and is faced with inadequate structures for the training of practitioners, for quality assurance and for statutory support.

In its underlying principles, the complementary therapies field is remarkably close to an Adult Education philosophy which is learner-centred, holistic and systemic.

The Government recognises the contribution of alternative therapies in enriching the lives of the many Adult Education participants in the area; in their contribution to expanding the concept of health and treatment and in the promise of the holistic, innovative approaches in working with people with disabilities or who are otherwise disadvantaged.

Notwithstanding the level of activity that the complementary therapies account for in the Adult Education sphere, it is outside the scope of a White Paper on Adult Education to address the specific organisational and developmental needs of the area. The recognition it is receiving in the context of this White Paper is to acknowledge the contribution it is making to the Adult Education field generally. Due to the growing significance of this area, the National Adult Learning Council will be asked to liaise with the National Qualifications Authority of Ireland, the Department of Health and Children, and practitioners to explore the feasibility of developing certification and accreditation processes for programmes in complementary therapies. The Department of Health and Children is hosting a Consultative Forum on this issue in the Autumn, and the output of this Forum can feed into the work of the National Adult Learning Council in this area.

Chapter 6
Workplace Education

CHAPTER 6
Workplace Education

6.1 LIFELONG LEARNING AND THE LABOUR MARKET

6.1.1 The European Commission has identified three sectors of low, medium and high job growth. Low growth or declining sectors are agriculture, manufacturing, mining and electricity/gas/water. These will become increasingly less important on the labour market.

Medium growth sectors are construction, distribution, transport, and communications, banking and insurance and public administration.

High growth sectors are found in the services areas, especially business related and personal services, health and recreation and education and training. Other than the hotel and catering areas, these are high skill areas.

The *ESRI/FÁS Manpower Forecasting Structures Report, No.7, –Aspects of Occupational Change in the Irish Economy: Recent Trends and Future Prospects (1998)*, a survey of emerging labour needs in the Irish economy, suggests that these general historic patterns are likely to prevail in the short to medium term in the Irish labour market.

The study predicts a fall off in employment in agriculture, labouring and some personal services. Large proportionate increases are predicted for professionals, managers, sales workers and catering. Generally, these trends indicate an increased demand for workers with third-level qualifications for service workers both high skilled and low skilled and a declining demand for unskilled manual workers and agricultural workers.

The study indicates that, notwithstanding labour shortages throughout the skill spectrum, it is likely that the pattern of rising educational attainment of the Irish labour force already well established will continue:-

Table 6:1

EDUCATIONAL ATTAINMENT OF THE IRISH LABOUR FORCE (%)

Highest Level Attained	1991-1995	1996-2000	2001-2005	2006-2010
Primary	21.8	16.2	12.2	9.5
Intermediate Cert.	26.2	24.6	22.7	20.3
Leaving Cert.	30.5	30.8	32.8	33.8
Third-level	21.7	28.4	32.3	36.7

As the above table shows, between 1991 and 2010 the proportion in the labour force with primary education as their highest level is expected to halve, while the proportion with third-level education will grow from one-fifth to over one-third. In general the ESRI has concluded that the labour market will be tight for skilled labour and semi-skilled labour with the only area of over-supply being amongst those with no qualifications.

6.1.2 A number of recent studies have shown that the Irish economy is already experiencing significant skills shortages (i.e. deficient in qualifications for particular jobs) and labour shortage (i.e. demand exceeding supply for workers prepared to work at the prevailing rates). Both the ESRI/FORFÁS (1998) and the Chambers of Commerce of Ireland (1999) in two separate studies have drawn attention to the difficulties which an increasing number of firms are having in filling vacancies, particularly for skilled staff in computer and engineering; crafts; clerical work and in the hotel and catering sector. In their most recent Economic Survey of Ireland (1999) the OECD noted that:-

> *"Labour shortages have moved beyond the realm of specific skills to a more generalised scarcity of even unskilled labour".*

This discussion suggests that a proactive lifelong learning policy focused on the labour market requirements of a competitive Irish economy would:-

- continue to focus on the labour market relevance of initial education and training;

- direct an increasing level of attention to the continuing education and training of those already at work;

- develop tailored programmes for groups wishing to re-enter the workforce, particularly for those with low educational levels; for women in the home, long-term unemployed or those aged over 60 currently out of the workforce or who may wish to re-enter it.

6.1.3 The first report of the *Expert Group on Future Skills Needs (1998)* highlighted emerging skills shortages in computer software, electronic and technician training, and in language skills for the teleservices sector. On foot of this, the Government committed a major investment aimed at increasing the supply of software graduates and technicians allied with investment in the PLC sector to promote training in teleservices and languages. The provision included:-

- £75m for 5,400 places for IT training in the third-level sector;

- 1,100 places aimed at mature students, the unemployed and workers in employment on an Accelerated Technician Programme in partnership with industry within the IoT sector;

- a further £6m towards the continued provision of 1,500 post-graduate IT conversion courses;

- £3.2m to enable FÁS to train an additional 700 people in relevant IT skills.

As a result significant progress has been made in implementing the recommendations of the Expert Group's first report.

The second report by the Group has been published recently focusing on the chemical and biological sciences areas, including Pharmaceuticals, Food, Biotechnology and Medical Devices, and research and construction crafts. It recommends: -

- an additional 1,150 places, phased over 4-5 years in life science courses in order to meet a projected shortfall of 290 graduates per annum;

- a range of actions to promote awareness and attractiveness of opportunities in the science field;

- the extension of the Accelerated Technician Programme, in partnership with the relevant companies by an additional 250 science technician students;

- a need to target researchers abroad to come to Ireland to meet expected shortfalls as well as financial support and awareness raising to improve the attractiveness of research as a career.

The Report estimates that an additional 16,000 skilled craftspersons in the construction sector will be needed by 2003, and that if the economy continues to grow at current rates, the actual skills shortage could be as high as 5,000 by 2003. It recommends:-

- that present blockages in the education sector element of apprenticeship training be removed;

- that the number of apprenticeships be increased;

- that a committee be established to examine the scope for shortening the duration of some apprenticeships, and providing routes to formal craft training for experienced but unqualified workers;

- and that initiatives be implemented to attract skilled workers from abroad.

In general, the report indicates that an additional 356,000 jobs are expected to be created in the next decade, and that the labour force will grow by 341,000 workers, with the greatest growth in the years immediately ahead. It highlights the need for labour market supply to be increased through encouraging re-entry to the workforce of women in the home, older persons, particularly over 55s, unemployed and social welfare recipients and their spouses. It welcomes developments in relation to providing childcare, but considers that further initiatives may be necessary, and recommends that employers increase the availability of flexible working time and location options. The work of the Group is now turning its attention to in-company training within the information technology and other sectors and will engage in further studies to ascertain the current level of such training, and to identify new approaches which many be needed to further augment the numbers undergoing enhanced skills training.

Female participation in the labour market rose to 46% by 1999, compared with 70.2% for males. Between 1993 and 1999 female participation in the 25-34 age group rose by 14.1% to 75.2%, and that in the 45-54 age group rose by 12.5 percentage points.

6.1.4 The National Competitiveness Council's *Annual Competitiveness Report 1999* identified technological innovation as the key-underlying determinant of structural change in the economy and called for increased investment in research, technical development and innovation. The Government has committed a sum of £1.95bn over the next seven years to meet the needs of this area. Two major elements of this investment provide for :-

- a £560m *Technology Foresight Fund*, launched by the Tánaiste and Minister for Enterprise, Trade and Employment to establish Ireland as a location for world class research excellence in niche areas, in the ICT and Biotechnology sectors. A dedicated Research Foundation is being established to evaluate research projects, and manage and allocate funding. The Foundation will put in place appropriate procedures for a competitive international peer review process. In an increasingly knowledge based society, competitive advantage will rest heavily on ensuring that Ireland becomes one of Europe's most attractive locations for knowledge-based, high-tech enterprise, both Irish and foreign owned;

- £550m (£281m for current and £269m for capital expenditure) to enhance the research, technological development and innovation capacity of the third-level education sector. This will strengthen the research, science and technology capability of higher education institutions, and facilitate collaborative efforts with industry to ensure an R&D culture in all sectors of the economy. The strengthening of graduate enterprise programmes and of higher education-industry links will be a priority in this measure.

The investment will also allow for the development of schemes of post-graduate and post-doctoral supports for researchers and will facilitate the expansion of peer reviewed project basic research. Inter-institutional co-operation will also be targeted to ensure critical mass at national level in key areas.

6.1.5 Lifelong learning is a central theme of the *National Employment Action Plan (NEAP) 2000* to address unemployment and social exclusion, and emerging skill and labour shortages through:-

- assisting unemployed people to return to work, by preventive interventions to minimise the duration of short-term unemployment and prevent the drift into long-term unemployment, and through systematic supports for those currently long-term unemployed;

- increasing participation in the labour market by improving employability and the incentive to work, increasing female participation, promoting equality of opportunity, and encouraging a balanced increase in immigration;

- enhancing the quality of labour supply and upgrading the skills of those in the workforce through continued investment in education and training and the development of a framework for lifelong learning;

- enhancing the responsiveness and relevance of the initial education system to ensure optimum participation in school to completion of upper secondary education.

6.1.6 Within the *Programme for Prosperity and Fairness (2000)*, the emphasis on competitiveness is on strengthening enterprise, including the small business and the services sector, promoting indigenous industry, addressing skill shortages, and accelerating e-Commerce and the information society. Strategies to upgrade the skills of those in the workforce, particularly those on low pay, the promotion of flexibility and family friendly policies, and increases in childcare provision are given priority. There is a particular focus on deepening partnership in the workplace, supporting new forms of work organisation and greater levels of employee participation, allied with investment in training and development to promote lifelong learning.

6.2 Learning Organisations

A highly skilled workforce, well educated and trained, is a pre-requisite for the maintenance of competitiveness and ensuring the capacity for adaptability and change. Within such an agenda there is a need for firms and workers both to develop the "soft" core skills such as attitude to work, initiative, a quality focus, communications, problem solving, team-working, flexibility and learning to learn, as well as the business and technical skills needed to keep up to date with best practice in changing product and process technology and production techniques. There is a need for firms to view such investment in human capital as being as important and planned for as investment in other aspects such as plant, machinery, new products and processes, on a par with firms of other European countries. The challenge of transforming the workplace into a learning organisation is arguably the ultimate goal of a workplace strategy. Longworth and Davies (1996) have identified the following characteristics of a learning organisation:-

- it invests in its own future through the education and training of all its people;

- it creates opportunities for its entire people in all its functions to reach their full potential;

- it works to a shared vision;

- it integrates work and learning;

- it empowers all people to broaden their horizons in harmony with their own preferred learning styles;

- it applies up-to-date open and distance education and training delivery technology so as to create broader and more varied training opportunities;

- it interacts proactively with the wider environment in which it operates;

- it is in a continuous state of learning so as to remain innovative and inventive. (1996, pp.75/59)

6.3 Partnership

6.3.1 The skill shortages that threaten current levels of economic growth in Ireland heighten the need for tailored responses and for active relationships between industry and education and training providers. While such relationships have emerged to meet the needs of industry, they can significantly benefit education establishments also. Economic growth and the labour demands which ensue from it can begin to compete with schools and colleges for personnel and can, paradoxically, make the decision to stay in, to re-enter or to continue in education less attractive not only to adults but to young second-level students also.

The Government is concerned at the possibility that learners would terminate or postpone their participation in education because of the attractions of paid employment. It is also concerned that those already in employment are likely to have even less opportunity for ongoing training and development because industry, already short-staffed, cannot release workers for such programmes.

The concept of education/training/workplace consortia has been pioneered through a number of European initiatives in recent years. Such consortia provide an attractive option in exploring workplace education/training in that:-

1. they allow for locally relevant, customised responses with the voluntary participation of all the stakeholders;

2. they allow for flexible delivery systems and for new routeways between work and education;

3. they lead to new synergies between education, training and the workplace;

4. they can facilitate sectoral as well as area-based responses;

5. they normalise the co-existence of education and training with work;

6. they allow for local developments within the context of a national framework.

6.3.2 Data supplied by IBEC, which were constructed from Revenue Commissioner information and other sources, give the following outline of firm size in Ireland:-

Table 6:2

NUMBER OF EMPLOYEES	NO OF COMPANIES	%
1-10	107,218	86%
11-50	14,012	11%
51-100	1,512	1.2%
101-500	1,099	0.88%
501+	293	0.23%

It is clear that while the larger companies will be in a position to fund and provide their own programmes for upskilling workers, the majority of small firms would find this difficult, and are likely to rely heavily on the education and training sector and other mechanisms to provide lifelong learning opportunities. One such measure is the *National Training Networks Programme* launched by the Department of Enterprise, Trade and Employment in 1999. This provides £12.7m over a 3-year period for employer-led training initiatives for small and medium sized enterprises. Of this, £1.7m will come from the European Social Fund, and at least £2m will be contributed by companies. The aim of the initiative is to develop sectoral networks to bridge the skills gap, so that groups of companies can share best practice, discuss common problems and pool resources towards purchasing or developing common training solutions. A company called *Skillnets Ltd.* has been established to oversee the programme. The programme covers companies ready to operate as a network, companies interested in developing a network, and research to explore common problems and identify solutions.

6.3.3 In addition, a *National Training Fund* is being established in conjunction with the removal of sectoral and apprenticeship levies which will be managed by the Department of Enterprise Trade and Employment and applied to a range of training programmes.

6.3.4 £5m is being made available by the Department of Enterprise, Trade and Employment to fund measures aimed at improving employment opportunities for people with disabilities. Of this, £4m will be for a new *Supported Employment Programme* that will provide employment for up to 750 people with disabilities in the open labour market. The remainder is for supports to employers to provide disability awareness training, and to provide for re-training employees who have acquired a disability in the course of their working lives.

The participation of employers at national level in national partnership agreements, in EU monitoring committees, in the Expert Group on Future Skills Needs, and in national curriculum and certification structures, is designed to ensure that national quality standards are set in line with best practice, that emerging training needs are identified, and that programmes maintain relevance to changing needs. IBEC's Business-Education Links Scheme and European Orientation Programmes, and the IT industry-led FIT (Fast Track IT) initiative also play a very positive role in this respect.

6.3.5 However, the need is also recognised for local education/training and industry partnerships, aimed at responding flexibly to local variations and priorities. A more fluid cross over from those in the workplace into training/education and from those in training/education into the workplace could be progressed through initiatives such as:-

- expanded industry and work placement opportunities for higher education institutions;

- agreements between industry and education on aspects such as timetabling and modularisation of course provision;

- recognition of learning in the workplace for accreditation and progressionpurposes;

- the delivery of courses in the workplace.

6.4 Paid Educational Leave

The Green Paper re-opened the debate on Paid Educational Leave - a topic which was much in vogue in the 1970s but, through the depressed years of the 1980s receded somewhat in public consciousness.

Submissions from different pillars to the *Programme for Prosperity and Fairness 2000* on the New Partnership Agreement stressed the importance of paid educational leave as a major systemic incentive to workers to undertake ongoing education and training. This issue will undoubtedly also surface in the context of the work of the Task Force on Lifelong Learning referred to later in this Chapter. Any developments in this area will need to incorporate a specific equality strategy, given the evidence in the International Adult Literacy Survey results for Ireland showing a marked disparity between the level of employer supports provided for males and females to enable them to access continuing education and training.

6.5 Flexible Education and Training

6.5.1 Given the constraints imposed by firm size in Ireland, promoting a widespread culture of lifelong learning will require a renewed focus by education and training providers on creating flexible options for those in the workforce to combine employment, learning and family responsibilities. This is especially necessary given the constraints on employers releasing staff for training in a climate of labour and skill shortages. There is an urgent need to increase the range of flexible learning options through increased use of distance learning, part-time courses, and sandwich and summer courses. The Back to Education Initiative will provide for a substantial increase in this area, allied with a national adult ICT skills programme. This needs to be accompanied by increased opportunities for mature student participation in third-level education, and the removal of barriers in this area. This is examined further in Chapter 7.

6.5.2 The *Task Force on Lifelong Learning* established by the Department of Enterprise, Trade and Employment in collaboration with the education sector will play particular attention to this area. The Task Force will explore:-

- the development of specific initiatives to upgrade the skills of workers in low paid sectors and those with low or obsolescent skills;

- supports, including information and advice, to assist people to identify learning opportunities appropriate to their needs and to source suitable learning opportunities;

- the enhancement of access to education and training with particular emphasis on financial issues, such as fees and educational leave, and on measures to support the reconciliation of learning and family life;

- increasing diversity and flexibility of provision and promoting the responsiveness of education and training institutions to the needs of adults, with particular attention being given to those who are disadvantaged;

- further development of linkages between firms and training and education institutions;

- initiatives to significantly increase training, learning and progression opportunities for people faced with the challenge of rapid technological change, taking due account of the work of the Expert Group on Future Skills Needs; and

- initiatives to help people currently outside the workforce to upgrade their skills and/or acquire new ones.

Wicklow County Council
County Library Services

6.6 Tax Relief

The utilisation of tax incentives to promote adult learning has been strongly advocated in the European *White Paper, Teaching and Learning: Towards the Learning Society (1995)*. While currently, employers can available of tax exemptions for many forms of education or training expenditure, and while tax relief is available for part-time third-level education and IT and language programmes in FÁS, it is now desirable that a uniform national approach be adopted based on:-

- treating *all* such investment in "human capital" by employers on the same basis for taxation purposes as other capital investment;

- providing tax relief for *all* participants for fees incurred in engaging in nationally certified learning programmes, irrespective of their location, duration and level.

It is recommended that a working group be established to explore the feasibility of such an approach, and examine the cost and administrative implications.

6.7 Accreditation of Prior Learning and Work-Based Learning

Virtually all submissions received in the Consultation Process welcomed the developments under the Qualifications (Education and Training) Act (1999) but stressed the urgency of developing streamlined nationally available mechanisms for accreditation of prior learning and work-based learning (APL and WBL). A number of providers and certification bodies have piloted the development of such approaches, notably FÁS, NCVA, and individual third-level colleges for specific courses. A number of conferences have been held to share practice and discuss experiences.

However, a common experience for many learners undergoing APL and WBL is that the process is a complex one, with considerable support and guidance needed in assembling a portfolio of evidence to demonstrate, to the satisfaction of accreditors, that prior learning and skills have been achieved. In retrospect, some participants felt that it might have been easier to follow an entire education programme, or complete the assignments which fellow students would have undertaken. Clearly for APL and WBL to be replicable and transparent for mass participation, a streamlining and simplification of processes is required in a way which reduces the labour intensity of the support and guidance needed, while enabling learners to negotiate a successful pathway.

The implementation of this type of system would further develop the key principles underpinning the Qualifications (Education and Training) Act (1999) of access, transfer and progression. This is integral to the development of a comprehensive 'lifewide' learning process in that it supplements and interweaves with the provision already available through the formal structure. This system could also be made available to community-based education programmes and would contribute significantly to the realisation of such sites as legitimate learning arenas. In a European context, the availability of a streamlined APL and WBL system would facilitate the recognition of learning for Irish workers seeking employment abroad, and for those seeking employment in Ireland from outside of the country.

There are many different outcomes of APL. Recognising previously acquired skills and competence will mean that the adult learner can:-

- achieve portable qualifications in a credentialist labour market, and can compete with those who have had the benefits of formal learning;

- gain access to courses of learning with specific entry level requirements;

- obtain exemption from units of particular courses of learning.

WBL allows for people in the workplace to engage in on-the-job training and development and have such learning accredited as a formal qualification or credit. However, many workplaces are not in a position to provide the types of guidance and assessment supports required by accredited learning.

In order to allow for APL and WBL to take place on a larger scale than to date, certification and assessment processes need to orientate their systems towards flexible forms of learning and assessment. In addition, systemised supports need to be made available to guide learners through these processes.

Learning and assessment systems that best enable APL and WBL have the following characteristics:-

- they are modular;

- they have an outcomes-based approach;

- they allow for credit accumulation over a period of time.

The availability of qualified learning assessors for APL and WBL, would greatly enhance provision in this area. This White Paper recommends that, among other options, the National Qualifications Authority of Ireland should explore, in collaboration with the National Adult Learning Council, the feasibility of a **national training programme to develop a pool of highly skilled Learning Assessors**. The programme would be targeted at education and training providers, those in supervisory and management positions in industry (including people who may no longer be active in the workforce), in order to develop the necessary skills. This approach would help develop, over time, a cadre of regionally-based experts in a position to support individual, WBL and APL mechanisms in a flexible manner.

The Learning Assessor would have the role of both guiding and assessing individual learners through the assessment process. Following training and a quality assurance process, successful Learning Assessors would be recognised by FETAC and HETAC. They could have their names published on a panel which could then be accessed through designated learning and assessment centres, on payment of a standard fee, by learners wishing to pursue this route to APL or WBL.

6.8 Community Employment

There are now some 36,800 people involved in the Community Employment Programme. This programme had its origin as a work placement programme primarily. In a situation approaching full employment and labour shortages, the Government has signalled its intention to reduce numbers on the CE scheme to 28,000 on a phased basis. Rising skills needs also strengthen the case for a heavier emphasis on education and training as part of the CE programmes. The National Adult Learning Council will work with FÁS in exploring ways in which CE participants can be encouraged to extend their education and training participation, both during their own time and in their sponsor's time.

Increased emphasis on the education and training component within Community Employment is part of a general strategy to increase progression opportunities into work or further learning for participants on work experience programmes. In addition, a re-allocation of resources from Community Employment on a phased basis is also planned to partially fund a dedicated Social Economy Programme to encourage the provision of a range of services along a continuum between commercial and statutory provision, particularly targeted at disadvantaged communities and long-term unemployed people. The programme will provide funding for three types of enterprise:-

- Community Businesses ultimately financed from trading income alone which would be expected to move into self-sustaining viability in the medium term;

- Deficient Demand Social Economy Enterprises where the demand for goods and services within a community is not matched by resources to pay for them, due to disadvantage or low density of population;

- enterprises based on public sector contracts, where public expenditure in disadvantaged communities is sub-contracted to local social economy enterprises.

White Paper on Adult Education – Learning for Life

6.9 New Entrants to the Workforce

A rapidly expanding workforce is recruiting workers at all skill levels. The Government is concerned that new entrants may be joining the workforce at the low skill end, poorly prepared for sectoral or economic downturn or for progressing their own careers. They are, therefore, vulnerable to unemployment and are limited in their career building prospects by a poor foundation in education and skill. It is desirable that those in such situations should not have to make a choice *between* work and education/training, but that there should be active education and training support for them in the work context. This will be a particular priority of the Task Force on Lifelong Learning in consultation with employers and trade unions.

The Trade Union Movement has a particular role to play in this area. Traditionally, the Trade Union Movement has been a major player in the education of workers. The educational activity of the Trade Unions has embraced agendas covering member development and organisational development matters, as well as direct vocational or technical training.

The experience and the expertise which the Trade Union Movement has acquired in the 1980s in working with the unemployed in education and training can now usefully be applied to working with the employed in a similar context. For this reason it is desirable that the trade unions' attention in this area be maximised.

Emerging developments, following the Educational Welfare Act 2000, will play an important role in this area. Under the Act, young people aged 16-18 who intend to leave school early will be required to register with the Educational Welfare Board being set up under the Act. The Board will draw up a plan for the further education and training of the individual concerned, and will require that person to make all reasonable efforts to carry out the plan. It is on this basis that the Board will issue a certificate entitling the young person to work, and it will not be possible for the a young person aged between 16 and 18 to be employed without a certificate.

6.10 Workplace Literacy

The continued expansion of the Adult Literacy Service will include a focus on expansion of workplace literacy initiatives in collaboration with industry. The National Adult Literacy Agency has trained a number of tutors to provide literacy in the workplace and has promoted the availability of the service among employer organisations. A pilot project has started in a large firm in the Dublin area, and similar initiatives are being planned for workers in the health and local authority sectors. These will be further expanded in the light of experience and evaluation of their effectiveness.

6.11 Languages

2001 will be designated the *European Year of Languages*. During that year information and promotional measures will be undertaken (at European, national, regional and local levels) with the aim of encouraging language learning throughout the EU. The key aim of the European Year of Languages will be to raise awareness of cultural diversity and to promote the advantages of competencies in a range of languages as a key element in personal development, in intercultural understanding and in enhancing the economic potential of individuals, enterprises and society as a whole. Language learning will be a particular priority within programmes under the Back to Education Initiative.

6.12 Technical Support

The promotion of opportunities for education and training of those in the work place will be a key priority of the National Adult Learning Council. A unit will be established within the Council to provide technical support and advice on initiatives and policies in this area, on an ongoing basis.

6.13 Conclusion

This chapter sets out a number of recommendations to support increased learning opportunities for those in the workplace. These include the development of industry/education/training partnerships, increased flexibility in education and training course delivery, a working group to explore tax relief for employer and participant outlay on further education and training, and expansion of workplace literacy initiatives. In addition, the National Qualifications Authority of Ireland will be asked to explore with the National Adult Learning Council the feasibility of establishing a pool of highly skilled Learning Assessors to support mechanisms for the accreditation of prior learning and work based learning.

White Paper on Adult Education – Learning for Life

Chapter 7
Higher Education

CHAPTER 7
Higher Education

7.1 The Green Paper and earlier chapters in this White Paper have drawn attention to the comparatively low levels of educational attainment of Irish adults, when compared with most other industrialised countries and also when compared with younger age groups in Ireland. This White Paper has proposed a multi-faceted range of initiatives in second chance and further education; in education in the community and in the workplace aimed at addressing these disparities. This chapter looks at the role which third-level institutions can play in this regard.

The *Report of Review Committee on Post-Secondary Education and Training Places (1999)* draws attention to the fact that the proportion of adults in the Irish population with at least upper second-level education is significantly below the OECD average:-

> *"The high proportion in the age cohort under review who do not have upper secondary education is striking. Many people in this age group would have chosen to participate in third-level education if they had the opportunity. It seems clear that the Leaving Certificate is still the critical gateway for further and higher education and training. The means by which adult learners can either access Leaving Certificate, or have alternative qualifications, for access, needs to be addressed." (P.59)*

The Committee went on to recommend an additional stock of up to 10,000 places for mature students, of which at least 80% should be part-time, *"which should be built up over a number of years. We recommend that before the places are provided, the demand is validated by appropriate market research on the target population to determine the extent of demand, the courses sought and the most appropriate method of provision".* The Report recommended that *"institutions, including all those providing distance education to Irish residents, should be invited to submit proposals for the provision of additional places for mature students to the Higher Education Authority."*

In Ireland, access to higher education is primarily through a narrow sequential pathway following school. There are limited opportunities for alternative entry points for adults generally in the system. This is one of the reasons why Ireland has amongst the lowest mature student participation in higher education in the industrialised world.

According to the OECD, *Education Policy Analysis (1997)*, just over 19% of new entrants to degree level programmes in all OECD countries in 1995[1] were aged 26 or over, compared to an Irish figure of 2%. With regard to Certificate and Diploma Level programmes, the OECD average was almost 37% compared to an Irish figure of just over 1%.

---

1. This data excluded entrants to part-time programmes and is therefore underestimated.

Demographic trends, particularly the fall-off in second-level school-leavers, may mean that pressure for places in third-level may begin to weaken in the immediate future. Optimism, however, that such a development would lead to a greater availability of mature students in higher education, should be qualified by a number of considerations. It has been argued in the consultation process that the fall-off in school leavers from second-level may not be as high or as protracted as currently envisaged, because of higher than anticipated rates of inward migration. At second-level, some 2,834 students entered the second-level education system from outside the State in 1999/2000, including 408 who entered PLC courses. Total enrolment from outside the State within the second-level system was 5,781, including 753 in PLC courses. The overall numbers from outside the State are distributed over a number of class years. In addition, immigration, currently averaging approximately 47,500 people annually, including dependants, is likely to increase considerably in the context of addressing labour shortages and skill needs.

The reduction in demand for third-level places may not be spread evenly throughout the third-level sector. Suppressed demand for University places for instance means that falling numbers of school- leavers are likely to affect the Universities last and least.

Considerations such as these tend to suggest that in the absence of positive discrimination in favour of mature students, the availability of places for mature students in higher education – particularly in the university sector – may not be as high as a preliminary examination of school leaving trends might indicate. The task of raising mature student participation in higher education in Ireland to levels similar to that of most other OECD countries poses a significant challenge for Government and for higher education institutions.

7.2 The *Report of the Commission on the Points System (1999)* sets targets for the establishment of quotas for mature students: 15% by 2005 and 25% by 2015. Additionally it calls for the establishment of a co-ordinated system of assessment of mature student applications by autumn 2002, and for a review of the definition of "part-time" courses. It also considers that a person who did not enter third-level education on leaving school should have access to the same financial support as a school-leaver, if he/she wishes to enter third-level education in later life, whether on a full-time or a part-time basis. It takes the view that:-

> *"The State has a responsibility to provide third-level places for adults who did not have access to third-level when they left school as well as having responsibility for providing third-level places for school leavers." (P.115)*

The Government recognises the major achievement of the third-level sector in Ireland in increasing overall participation five-fold since 1965/66. It also recognises that the sector will need significant support if it is to increase mature student participation not merely as an arbitrary add-on in a small number of departments but reflecting a core strategic shift in these institutions towards a lifelong learning mission.

7.3 Key Directions

7.3.1 Wagner has identified four key directions for higher education policy as it embarks on such a strategic shift towards a commitment to lifelong learning:-

- the relationship between higher education institutions and the learner extending over the lifetime based on a policy which welcomes rather than deflects demand;

- new approaches to standards and qualifications focused on greater clarity and transparency in the intended outcomes of study programmes;

- expanded partnerships and links across sectors and levels of education, i.e. between education and work and between third and second-level education;

- new approaches to securing and using finance, drawing on resources from a multiplicity of sources, both public and private and shifting funding to an outcomes basis.   (Wagner, 1999)

7.3.2 Such a strategic shift by higher education institutions in Ireland would involve policy changes on many fronts. Amongst the most urgent of these would be:-

- establishing targets at institutional level across faculties and disciplines for full-time and part-time mature student enrolments in line with national targets;

- recognising the need for much greater flexibility by those institutions in:-

ACCESS AND DELIVERY

- timing - part-time/full-time mix;

- modularisation of programmes;

- semesterised delivery;

- off-campus provision;

- expanding the range of delivery modes and adopting more adult friendly pedagogies and a culture of transparency and dialogue;

- recognition of a range of access routes and qualifications;

- provision and/or recognition of access programmes to the extent needed;

- development of outreach strategies and distance delivery;

- implementation of an equality strategy to promote and monitor the participation of specific groups;

- data-gathering mechanisms which support evaluation and analysis of recruitment, participation and progression trends for specific groups;

- networking between colleges to share good practice and develop mainstream co-ordinated approaches.

ASSESSMENT AND ACCREDITATION

- procedures for accrediting prior learning;

- recognition of the non-linear nature of adult learning;

- transparent mechanisms for inter-institutional credit transfer and accumulation, within and across levels, sectors and the binary divide;

- wider range of assessment procedures, incorporating a clearer outcomes focus;

- ensuring that criteria concerning equality issues are adhered to in extending mature student participation;

- expansion of single module certification where appropriate.

- educational information and guidance services, appropriate to the needs of adults and school leavers;

- counselling and pastoral care services;

- additional mentoring, tuition and group support as needed;

- childcare facilities for parent participants;

- full access to college library, IT, sport and social facilities.

Above all,there is a need for a co-ordinated and consistent strategy across colleges, which confers a range of entitlements for adults as part of a structured national approach.

7.4 Programme for Prosperity and Fairness

In that context, the *Programme for Prosperity and Fairness 2000* makes a number of commitments: -

"Places will be provided to support access by mature students to third-level education, allied with the promotion of "adult-friendly" policies.

A Group will be established, with appropriate social partner involvement, to examine and report on barriers to participation by mature students in higher education. The Group will advise the Department of Education and Science on the development of a co-ordinated framework to promote access by mature and disadvantaged students to third-level education, building on the experience of current initiatives.

Participation by disadvantaged groups in third-level education will be encouraged through the provision of significant additional investment. Flexible entry, delivery and accreditation arrangements, linkages with second-level schools, actions to promote mature student participation, and outreach, community education and support programmes will form part of the approach. Access, transfer and progression will be actively promoted within the context of the National Qualifications Framework.

Additional financial supports for disadvantaged students, including disadvantaged mature students, will be put in place, targeted at those most in need.

A Study will be finalised of completion rates in Universities and Institutes of Technology, which will make recommendations on how best to improve participation and retention within the third-level sector. This will include initiatives to encourage female take-up in non-traditional disciplines. The views of the social partners will be sought on the findings of the study.

Both the Points Commission and the Review Committee on Post-Secondary Education and Training Places noted the lack of information about demand from mature students. The Higher Education Authority has been requested to undertake market research to establish the level and range of demand from mature students. In the light of the outcome of this research, measures will be designed to meet mature student demand and ensure flexible, innovative responses to mature students' needs for consideration by Government. These measures will be based on the recommendations of the Points Commission and the Review Committee's Report.

Colleges will aim to provide that, by 2005, 15% of intake each year will comprise students aged 23 or over. A cross-faculty approach will be promoted and in the light of the outcomes of the research mentioned above, individual faculty targets will be set. Increasing the mature student intake over the next 5 years, in line with the Review Committee's recommendations, will involve increased part-time provision and other flexible options, such as distance learning opportunities."

7.5 Targeted Higher Education Mature Student Fund

A Targeted Higher Education Mature Student Fund will be established to promote institutional and co-ordinated change aimed at increasing mature student participation and benefit from third-level education at under-graduate level, particularly for those who do not have the necessary points under the Leaving Certificate. The fund will be a competitive one, to be disbursed on the basis of national criteria to institutions that display institution-wide directional shifts along the lines advocated in the Paper. Cross faculty approaches, partnerships with other colleges and/or accrediting bodies, and participation in networks to share results, good practice and agree a mainstreaming strategy where appropriate, will be part of the requirements. A key focus on the fund will be on increasing participation of disadvantaged mature students in third-level education. The phased increase in the fund should be linked to validated demand, underpinned by the market research which is being carried out at present in relation to mature student demand generally.

Progress in individual colleges should be monitored by the Academic Councils and reported to the HEA, which should compile a composite national report on the measure on a twice-yearly basis.

The fund for this purpose will increase on a phased basis to £10m per annum, and should embrace under-graduate degree programmes, nationally certified short or modularised courses (including in the universities), nationally certified distance learning courses and access courses which carry an entitlement to entry. The Fund will apply to specific pre-approved initiatives and courses which will be linked to certification, and which offer progression routes to higher education. Consideration will also be given in that context to the promotion of progression routes from Apprenticeships to higher levels of education and training within the Institutes of Technology.

7.6 Distance Education

There are currently two main providers of distance education opportunities in Ireland - The National Distance Education Centre - OSCAIL - and the Open University. About 7,000 students are currently pursuing undergraduate and post-graduate programmes with these two bodies. The number of students on under-graduate courses enrolled in the National Distance Education Centre, DCU has risen from a figure of 940 in 1988 to 2,806 in 1997, a growth of 198% over the last nine years. There is clearly, a robust demand for this form of educational participation.

The National Distance Education Centre was established as a collaborative structure of higher education and other providers in the State in the early 1980s. The Centre was established as the service arm of the National Distance Education Council, a representative body of providers but established as a sub-committee of the Governing Authority of DCU.

The inter-institutional collaboration involved in the work of the Centre has ensured that the development of distance education within this structure has proceeded in an agreed and systematic way; duplication has been avoided and the cost structure has been remarkably favourable by international standards.

There have, however, been some problems in the development of provision. Firstly the location of the National Centre within one institution may have contributed to reluctance in other colleges to undertake initiatives in this area, and to uncertainty as to the supports which will be available for such initiatives. Secondly, while some State funds are provided towards the operational costs of the National Distance Education Centre, the bulk of the costs are met from student fees. Such students are not counted for purposes of budgetary allocations to colleges, nor do they receive any form of State subvention themselves, other than in the form of tax relief.

Given the developments in new technology, the constraints on third-level infrastructure, the plans for a dedicated educational television channel, and the need to substantially increase mature adult participation through flexible options which can be combined with family and work responsibilities, it is an imperative that the scope for distance learning provision be used to full advantage.

The Higher Education Authority and OSCAIL jointly hosted a Symposium on the Future of Open and Distance Learning in Higher Education in Ireland in March 2000. The HEA has been asked to undertake a review of the provision of distance education in the light of the *Report of the Review Committee on Post-Secondary Education and Training Places (1999)*, chaired by Dr Donal de Buitléir. The market research on mature student demand which the Authority has also been asked to undertake will also contribute to progress in this area.

The National Adult Learning Council and the Higher Education Authority will be asked to work closely to progress this important area. A particular priority will be to explore mechanisms to provide financial support for initial course development work targeted at strategic areas, maximising the use of ICT and broadcasting in delivery.

7.7 Student Support

The task of raising mature student participation rates in Ireland involves supporting institutions as they make strategic shifts to support a culture of lifelong learning. The second aspect of this issue concerns the financial supports that would be available to mature students progressing through higher education.

The current Higher Education student schemes provide for free fees for EU nationals, refugees, and those with humanitarian leave to remain in the State, provided they satisfy a residency clause and are pursuing nationally certified undergraduate full-time programmes of at least two years' duration in recognised colleges. Means-tested maintenance grants are also available, and arrangements have been introduced to enable mature students to be paid the "away" rate of grant, irrespective of their distance from college. In contrast, part-time students receive no supports other than tax relief.

The consultation process arising from the Government Green Paper argued strongly for the abolition of part-time fees for third-level education. The cost of such a move would exceed £30m annually. In view of the high absolute costs of such an initiative; the risk of dead-weight and displacement investment where fees are frequently paid for by employers and the concern to direct resources to the most needy, the Government is not in a position to provide for free fees for part-time students at this stage. However, **arrangements will be implemented so that Higher Education fees will not apply to part-time students, who satisfy the residency clause, and who are social welfare means-tested or unemployment payment recipients or dependants, medical card holders or dependants, persons in receipt of Family Income Supplement or dependants.** These arrangements will apply to students who are pursuing:-

- a first degree;

- a first-time nationally certified certificate or diploma programme in a recognised college, including the university sector;

- a nationally certified third-level first-time distance learning programme in Ireland;

- a first -time access course that guarantees entry to further progression within the sector as recommended by the Points Commission.

The categories of beneficiary will be students or dependants in receipt of the payments set out for Category 2 under the Back to Education Initiative in Chapter 4.

In ring-fencing the scheme in this way, the Government believes that it can positively discriminate in favour of the most deserving groups economically; reach the most educationally disadvantaged sectors within the mature student population and respond in a very tangible way to the educational needs of those with the lowest incomes.

7.8 Monitoring Implementation

The Government is committed to increasing mature student participation in higher education in line with the recommendations of the *Report of the Review Committee on Post Secondary Education and Training Places (1999)* and the market research to be carried out on demand for places. Through the package of proposals outlined in this White Paper it is confident that the target of mature student entrants of 15% by 2005 can be met and that further increases can be achieved in subsequent years. To ensure the careful evaluation of progress towards these targets, the HEA will be asked on annual basis to monitor progress towards these goals and to propose remedial actions where the rate of progress is less than desired.

7.9 Conclusion

This chapter highlights the attention given in recent policy reports to the issue of mature student participation in higher education, and sets out the institutional and system changes which would support the development of adult friendly policies. A competitive Targeted Higher Education Mature Student Fund is recommended, rising on a phased basis to £10m per annum, to promote institutional and co-ordinated change in third-level colleges aimed at increasing mature student participation in higher education. The funds would be awarded, on the basis of national criteria to be developed in consultation with third-level interests, to institutions which display institution wide strategic directional shifts along the lines highlighted in the Paper. A general programme of free fees for part-time students is not advocated. However, fees will be abolished for persons on nationally certified part-time third-level courses who are medical card holders, recipients of the welfare/health payments or Family Income Supplement set out for Category 2 in the Back to Education Initiative (Chapter 4). This arrangement will also apply to dependants in this Category.

This Paper recognises the critical need to use the scope for distance learning provision to full advantage. The HEA, which is currently undertaking a review of distance education, will be asked to work with the National Adult Learning Council in progressing this important area. A particular priority will be to explore mechanisms to provide financial support for initial course development work targeted at strategic areas, maximising the use of ICT and broadcasting in delivery.

White Paper on Adult Education – Learning for Life

Chapter 8
Support Services

CHAPTER 8
Support Services

8.1 Training of Adult Educators

8.1.1 If the Adult Education sector is to make the quantum leap envisaged for it in this White Paper, it can only do so on the basis of a highly trained corps of adult educators and trainers who are dynamic and equipped to lead change, to play a key role in the policy debate and to reflect the distinctive identity of the sector in the field of professional practice and research.

The Green Paper presented a strong case for :-

- the development of recognised qualifications for the teaching and practice of Adult Education;

- structures for ongoing inservice training and career progression for practitioners;

- a Forum for Practitioners of Adult and Community Education.

This is not an attempt to segregate the provision of Adult Education from other forms of provision, or to exclude practitioners in other areas of education from practising in the Adult Education field. Rather, it is a question of widening the existing mechanisms for recognition of qualifications in education and training to embrace a variety of new qualifications in this field, and of providing mechanisms for accreditation of the learning of many practitioners in the sector who have considerable expertise and experience, but who lack formal qualifications. It is also a question of promoting teaching strategies appropriate to adults as a key element in the evolution of a framework for lifelong learning.

A growing number of employment opportunities have arisen in the adult and further education and training sector in recent years. Organisations such as FÁS, NRB and associated agencies, VECs, CERT, Teagasc, the burgeoning Community sector, the Prison Service, Employers, Trade Unions and voluntary bodies are involved in Adult Education and provide employment for adult educators. While it is essential that Adult Education retain the flexibility and freedom to draw from a wide range of sources and expertise, it is vital that, over time, qualifications for the teaching and practice of Adult Education be accorded formal recognition. This process needs to recognise the diversity of the sector and provide for the multiplicity of actors and providers in the field.

Significant work in this area has already been undertaken by FÁS, both in the training of their trainers, in the registration of approved trainers and in leading the establishment of a trainers' network. In recent years the NRB, in association with NUI Maynooth has developed a programme for the training of tutors of people with disabilities. The Irish Institute for Training and Development has played a significant organisational and support role for trainers mainly within the business sector. In addition the Department of Education and Science has funded national certificate and diploma programmes in the field of vocational education and training provided on an inservice basis primarily for staff in Youthreach, Senior Traveller Training Centres and in the Adult Literacy Service.

These programmes have evolved with the support of the statutory bodies who are involved in adult learning provision. They embrace diverse modes of delivery, especially in the use of distance education methodologies, and are predominantly of an inservice rather than a pre-service nature.

8.1.2 **The Government recognises the need to explore the feasibility of developing a generic training programme in this field, to be implemented initially in a modular format on an inservice basis, but ultimately to be available as a pre-service training programme for the sector. As a first step, an inter-agency Working Group is recommended to progress the issue of formal recognition of qualifications for Adult Education practitioners.** This working group would need to: -

- represent the wide range of agencies in the field;

- examine the range of qualifications currently available in relation to the needs of the sector;

- identify generic training needs as well as the scope and need for specific specialisms on an elective basis;

- explore with relevant third-level colleges the scope for a modular and flexible approaches to the development of nationally certified inservice and pre-service training programmes;

- make recommendations on the future recognition of qualifications in the Adult Education sector.

Given the diffused range of interests involved in the sector, it will be essential to progress this work on a phased basis, underpinned by an inclusive participative consultation process, systematic research and a review of best international practice in this area.

8.1.3 Practitioners who lack Third-level Qualifications

Many of those employed in the Adult Education field have been recruited on the basis of a second-level teaching qualification or a trade or business qualification. While a number of them will have taken a variety of orientation and other programmes relating to working with adults, they will not, in most cases, have been accorded professional recognition for this. Many with an Adult Education qualification, but who lack a "teaching" qualification, may find it impossible to secure stable employment in their chosen field. There are also many workers in the community and voluntary sector with expertise and experience in this area but who lack the professional recognition of a formal qualification.

So as to ensure parity of esteem between the professionals within the education sectors, the Government envisages that the qualification as an adult educator will be a third-level one. There was general agreement with this view within the consultation process on the Green Paper.

As noted earlier there was some concern that professionalising the sector would result in the displacement of the high levels of high quality voluntary input in areas, for instance, such as adult literacy and Community Education. Equally there was concern that it would displace the many who, though lacking a teaching qualification, already possess the expertise and the innate pedagogical skills to work effectively with adults in a learning situation.

The Government is anxious to respond to this concern. It recognises the unique and invaluable contribution made by volunteers in the development of a sector where many elements have received little State funding or support to this point. It is concerned, therefore, not only that this contribution would be retained in the future, but that it be validated and acknowledged for its unique contribution. People working in the field who currently lack a qualification will be facilitated to attain certification through in-work education, block release and in-service opportunities. Those who are active as volunteers in their own communities should be provided with the opportunity to upgrade their knowledge, attitude and skills and to gain certification through flexible procedures.

The working group alluded to above will look specifically at the qualification needs and routeways of practitioners who lack a qualification. While not wishing to pre-empt the work of this group, it is likely, in following the principles elaborated upon elsewhere in this White Paper, to make provision for the accreditation of prior learning, workplace-based learning, community learning and criterion-referenced assessment.

8.2 Staff Development

The role played by professional bodies and associations in affirming the professional status of the members, in enhancing their members' individual and collective capacity and in contributing to debate and policy making of the sector with which they are respectively associated, is widely recognised. Such associations are highly significant in securing and enhancing the distinct identity of the sector with which they are associated. The fact that there is no forum in which adult and community educators can come together as a distinct and recognised professional group is a major deficit in laying down solid foundations for the ongoing development of the field. The National Adult Learning Council will therefore by asked to establish a **Forum for Adult Education Practitioners** which will:-

- provide an opportunity for the exchange of ideas and the sharing of good practice;

- provide a mechanism for new thinking and innovation in the field;

- enable practitioners to inform policy development;

- contribute to the development of solidarity and peer support amongst practitioners.

Increased and systematic investment in staff development is an essential part of the strategy to promote quality assurance within Adult Education, as well as a critical strand in supporting the evolution of a national qualifications framework. A dynamic range of initiatives are already under way across many of the programmes in the education and training sector, but their effectiveness and attractiveness is hampered to some extent by the lack of formal accreditation arrangements, and by their origins as ad hoc reactive developments. While there will be a continued need for short informal programmes to meet changing needs, there are distinct advantages in developing a modular sequential series of graded programmes leading to a nationally certified professional qualification. The flexibility of availing of single module certification that may be accumulated over time to a full award would be an important part of this approach. In addition, such an approach would ensure that new learning reflecting best practice is embedded on an ongoing basis into the formal body of professional practice and research in this field.

8.3 Career Paths for Practitioners

The Green Paper recognised the importance of developing career structures and conditions of employment in the Adult Education and training sector which reward excellence and professionalism, and which ensure the retention of expertise in the system for the future benefit of the sector and its participants.

While there has been some progress in this area since the Green Paper, there are still specific funding arrangements that result in protracted periods on short-term unstable employment for many in the field. These issues will be addressed in the period ahead in consultation with staff interests, and within the context of public service pay parameters. A key need will be to ensure the attractiveness of the profession while preserving its flexibility and adaptability.

Labour shortages throughout the economy have to some extent shifted the burden of proof of attractiveness from the employee to the employer. If the Adult Education sector is to continue to attract the high quality practitioner that it has so far succeeded in doing, the sector must now recognise that it is in competition with many other potential employers, both in the public and private domains, and must respond accordingly.

8.4 Assessment and Accreditation

8.4.1 Real commitment to a strategy of lifelong learning raises fundamental questions about the nature of learning, and the validation of such learning. The "lifewide" nature of lifelong learning accepts the reality of learning in a multiplicity of sites and through multiple sources. The learner centred aspect of its commitment involves a recognition of the learner as possessing a range of different intelligences - cognitive, social, physical, emotional and aesthetic - all of which must be engaged if the person is to grow to his/her full potential.

The Green Paper drew attention to the need for a national framework for accreditation and certification that would:-

- rely on a set of transparent and multi-faceted standards;

- recognise and award achievement based on multiple intelligences;

- be capable, through a set of objective and broadly based criteria, of assessing a wide range of learning;

- embody a variety of assessment modes, including portfolios, oral, aural, project-based etc;

- able learners to join a programme at different points on the route, depending on their other learning and qualifications, or to arrive at the same qualification from a multiplicity of backgrounds;

- on learning outcomes as well as on learning processes;

- be suitable for implementation in a wide variety of settings, including formal and informal education and training, and work-based training;

- be available flexibly and frequently, in line with learners' needs.

The Paper drew attention to lack of availability of systems for the accreditation of learning in the workplace and in the community. With regard to the latter, a recent report, *Towards an Integrated Accreditation Framework* (Lennon, 1999) considers that in those instances where community learning has been validated by mainstream institutions:-

> *"The accreditation process is time-consuming and costly. To date, the process has been dominated by mainstream values and principles (e.g. competition, individualism, focused on limited range of intelligences). As such, it is neither accessible nor appropriate to the learning programmes being run in the community and voluntary sector" (P.8)*

8.4.2 Since the publication of the Green Paper the Government has proceeded with the enactment of the legislation for the establishment of a National Qualifications Authority of Ireland to develop a national qualifications framework for non-university vocational education and training awards at further and higher levels. The role of the Authority is to establish the policies and criteria on which the framework will be based, provide a system for co-ordinating and comparing education and training awards, be a guarantor of quality, and promote and facilitate access, transfer and progression.

The Act also provides for the establishment of two councils, (the Further Education and Training Awards Council (FETAC) and the Higher Education and Training Awards Council (HETAC)) to determine the standards of knowledge skill or competence to be acquired by learners, to establish and publish the policies and criteria for the making of awards and the validation of programmes, to make or recognise awards, and to monitor and evaluate the quality of programmes.

The Act provides for an all-embracing network of relationship between providers in the further and higher education and training sectors, including a legislative requirement on the universities to cooperate with the new structures. The development of a national qualifications framework is a fundamental ingredient in a comprehensive system of lifelong learning.

8.4.3 This White Paper recommends that:-

- particular priority be given to the development of processes for the accreditation of learning in the workplace and the community;

- the feasibility of training and establishing panels of Learning Assessors, and of designated assessment centres, as suggested in Chapter 6 be explored to assist in this process;

- the National Qualifications Authority of Ireland be represented on the National Adult Learning Council to ensure an integrated approach to the implementation of the overall strategy in this critical area.

8.5 Adult Guidance and Counselling

8.5.1 The Concept

Guidance refers to a range of activities designed to assist people to make choices about their lives and to make transitions consequent on these choices.

In the context of adult education, this range of activities includes:-

- **Information** – providing clients with objective and factual data on the self, education and training courses, occupations, labour market information, entitlements;

- **Assessment** – helping clients to obtain a structured understanding of their own development;

- **Advice** - making suggestions based on the advisor's own knowledge and experience;

- **Counselling** – helping clients to explore their thoughts and feelings on their present situation, the choices open to them, and the consequences of those choice;

- **Teaching/Careers Education** – providing a programme of planned experiences to develop in clients the skills and knowledge to make decisions and transitions, e.g. job search;

- **Placement** – helping clients to achieve entry to a particular job or course;

- **Advocacy** – negotiating with companies, agencies, institutions on behalf of clients, especially those for whom there are barriers to access;

- **Feedback** – giving feedback to providers about the unmet needs of the client;

- **Follow-up** – contacting former clients to see what has happened to them and what further needs they may have;

- **Networking** – building links with employers, relevant agencies and institutions to enhance guidance work with clients;

- **Managing** – managing guidance activities into a coherent programme;

- **Innovating systems change** – supporting change in curricula, institutional and guidance practice to maintain and improve quality of guidance provision.

8.5.2 Current Provision

The Green Paper placed key emphasis on the importance of developing support services, such as guidance, so that adults can gain optimum benefit from a return to education relevant to their needs. The Paper acknowledged that there was no system of guidance and counselling services to meet adult needs in the education sector and recommended the development of a service which would cover a spectrum of needs ranging from initial outreach, particularly in the fields of literacy and basic education, vocational information, guidance and orientation, advice in dealing with learning fears, as well as counselling and access to expert services for those in need.

The post-primary school guidance service provides for the appointment of 2 guidance counsellors in schools of 1,000 or more pupils, 1.5 staff in schools of 800-1,000, 1 staff member for schools in the 500-800 range, and a half-time post for schools in the 250-500 range. Smaller schools get a provision in the form of part-time hours, subject to a minimum of 8 hours per week. To the extent that VTOS programmes operate in school settings, they may benefit, together with PLC programmes, from this provision.

As part of the mid-term review of EU Structural Funds 1994-1999, additional funds were provided by the European Social Fund for the development of a guidance, counselling and psychological service measure to cater for Youthreach, Community Training Workshops and Traveller Training Centre programmes for early school-leavers. This is complemented by a FÁS advocate service and both initiatives have now been mainstreamed as a core part of provision for this group.

In third-level education, the *Final Report and Recommendations of the Commission on the Points System (1999)* highlighted the submissions the Commission received on the lack of guidance and counselling for mature students interested in applying for Higher E ducation courses. The Report recommended that colleges should bear in mind the needs of mature students in the preparation of information for potential applicants. In addition, it recommended the development of a co-ordinated system of assessment of mature student applications under the CAO by Autumn 2002, in consultation with adult education and training and community education interests and the National Qualifications Authority of Ireland. The Report supported the recommendations on the establishment of a comprehensive guidance service for adults which would complement existing services and avoid duplication, and proposed that a freephone information line on education opportunities should form part of the approach.

FÁS provides a range of Training and Employment Services for unemployed persons, employers and communities. At any one time, its training services cater for some 18,000 participants, while its work experience programmes cater for a further 39,000. The FÁS Employment Service supports include the provision of labour market information, advice, vocational counselling, and job placement. The services also include:-

- notification of employer vacancies to FÁS – this is being used increasingly. In 1999, some 70,000 vacancies were notified to FÁS Employment Services. These vacancies are put on display in FÁS Employment offices for viewing by unemployed job seekers;

- registration of job seekers for referral to jobs advertised or entry onto training and labour market programmes;

- registration of job seekers seeking work in Europe through Eures (European Employment Services).

FÁS Employment Services are provided through a network of 134 Locations, including 54 full-time offices. FÁS has a client database linked to Department of Social, Community and Family Affairs Live Register database. FÁS also supports employment services through 95 Community organisations around the country.

For the unemployed / job seeker FÁS provides a guidance and information service in relation to employment, education and training opportunities. Details on all labour market opportunities can be accessed through the FÁS Client Database and caseload management system, which is available in all FÁS and Local Employment Service Locations. A Career Guidance database is also available which provides a compilation of information, and occupational trends of specific careers. This database has recently been updated to provide information on about 300 careers and is also available on CD-ROM and floppy disc.

The FÁS Employment Service is playing a central role in the implementation of the activation strategy set out in the National Employment Action Plan (see Chapter 2) by providing for a systematic engagement of the employment services with the unemployed. When persons are referred to FÁS they receive an action planning interview (s) which will be followed up by support onto a training or education programme or work opportunity. Work in this area is also supported through a network of Jobs Clubs, which were expanded by 5,200 places in 1999.

The Local Employment Service (LES) was established by Government in twenty-seven areas of high disadvantage to provide a gateway for long-term unemployed persons within these areas to access the full range of guidance, training, educational employment support opportunities available to help them obtain employment. A special Unit has been set up within FÁS to provide technical support to the Local Employment Service. The Local Employment Service is to be assimilated into FÁS in the current year, while ensuring that its unique partnership and integrated character, its responsiveness to local needs and its ethos and processes are maintained and enhanced. FÁS, the Local Employment Service and the Area-Based Partnerships operate closely with education and adult literacy providers, and with a range of youth, community and welfare services.

The growth and consolidation of developments in the Employment Services is playing a key role in improving the range of services available for job seekers. In proposing the development of an adult educational guidance service, the need is recognised to ensure integrated linkages with existing services, and concentrate efforts on those who have made a decision to enrol or are already enrolled on an adult education programme.

8.5.3 Recent developments in Adult Educational Guidance

A number of developments have taken place:-

- in 1998 the National Centre for Guidance in Education published a report *"Guidance in Adult and Continuing Education"* setting out the need for a service. It made recommendations on the services which should be provided and the principles which should underpin it, and highlighted examples of good practice in the UK.

- a training programme in the Educational Management of Adult Guidance has been developed and is being operated through a collaboration of the National Centre for Guidance in Education, NUI Maynooth and Marino Institute of Education. It is aimed at practitioners in a range of adult education and training settings and is designed to equip them with the knowledge and skills needed to develop, manage and critically evaluate adult guidance provision in their own organisations.

- Phase 1 of a pilot programme in Adult Educational Guidance, involving 10 projects, has started early this year aimed at supporting participants in VTOS, adult literacy, adult and community education programmes. It is overseen by an advisory group which is led by the National Centre for Guidance in Education, and includes participation from employer, trade union, educational, FÁS, employment service/area partnership and community and voluntary sector interests.

8.5.4 NATIONAL ADULT GUIDANCE AND COUNSELLING SERVICE

In the context of current provision, it is now proposed to put in place a National Adult Guidance and Counselling Service. £35m is being provided for this service and for staff development and programme support initiatives over the period of the National Development Plan 2000-2006. The service will include personal, educational and career guidance and will cover the pre-entry, entry, on-going and pre-exit stages. It will be underpinned by the following principles:-

- learner/client-centredness;
- confidentiality;
- impartiality;
- equal opportunities;
- accessibility;
- transparency;
- empowerment.

There is a number of integrated steps which must be taken to develop an effective service and to deal with gaps in the current provision. These include:-

- the provision of comprehensive information on adult learning opportunities in a format which is accessible to all. The wide range of providers in the field of adult education and training, and the frequency of changing course options, has contributed to fragmentation and considerable confusion in this area;

- the scope for developing national specifications and standards for a national website of learning opportunities, which can be locally updated and accessed on a local, institutional, sectoral or programme basis will be explored;

- the co-ordination, coherence and streamlining of access arrangements for mature students into third-level already highlighted by the Points Commission;

- provision of a telephone helpline service, as well ICT information points in libraries and community education services;

- provision of training in front line guidance and counselling skills for staff across the adult education and training sector;

- building on initiatives under YOUTHSTART and the FÁS NUI Maynooth programme, the development of a framework for qualifications in vocational training and professional development, enabling systemised training to be provided for the front line and specialist staff in the field;

- expansion of core adult guidance and counselling staff on a phased basis until a comprehensive service is available and provision of necessary ICT and other supports for the service;

- which would identify and share best practice, provide technical support and development, and monitor and evaluate the effectiveness of the service. It is envisaged that the National Centre for Guidance in Education, working closely with the National Adult Learning Council, will play a critical role in this area. The adult educational guidance service will co-ordinated and managed locally, and networked with other providers, by the Local Adult Learning Boards.

These issues will be progressed over the coming period in the context of funds provided under the National Development Plan. In relation to Higher Education, the availability of information, counselling and guidance services to adults will be among the criteria governing access of institutions to the Targeted Mature Student Access Fund.

8.5.5 Level of Service

Almost 210,000 adults are currrently availing of programmes in adult literacy, community education, VTOS, PLC, and self-funded part-time programmes. The emerging adult guidance service will not be in a position to address all their needs. Therefore the priorities will be:-

a) provision of a coherent information base which can be self-accessed by learners, allied with a helpline;

b) initial consultations with a trained adviser to help clarify needs, indicate appropriate pathways and/or referral;

c) more specialised support such as counselling (career, educational or personal) and assessment;

d) referral to psychological services where needed.

The first two levels, a) and b), will constitute a foundation level of service which will be available to all. The next two levels, c) and d), will be provided free to participants on adult literacy, VTOS and Youthreach programmes, and for participants entitled to free fees or a reduction to 30% under the Back to Education Initiative. For the remainder, it is envisaged that fees will be charged should they wish to avail of specialised support. All Adult Education providers are encouraged to develop a policy on Adult Education guidance, taking into account the framework provided in this paper.

Within the overall spectrum of needs, it is envisaged that some participants with acute needs may require referral to a psychological service. This service is available for participants on early school leaver programmes. The initial focus of the National Educational Psychological Service is on the needs of students in first and second-level schools, and the target is that all schools will have access to a service by 2004. At that stage, it is expected that the integration of provision for adults needs into the service will be explored. In the interim, a solution for participants who need specialised support may lie in the provision of flexible funds to the emerging guidance services for external referral to private practitioners. The focus of the work of the National Educational Psychological Service and of the developments outlined above is on meeting the *educational* needs of learners. Other counselling and psychological services will continue to be a matter for the Department of Health and Children.

8.6 Quality Assurance – Role of the Inspectorate

Arising from a period of widespread debate, in-depth examination and review, a number of educational reforms have been initiated in the Irish education system, culminating in the introduction of the Education Act (1998) in which a legal framework has been provided for the first time.

In the Education Act the Minister is charged with the responsibility of ensuring ... *"that there is made available to each person...a level and quality of education appropriate to meeting the needs and abilities of that person."*

The provision of Adult and Continuing Education services in Ireland has grown very rapidly and in very diverse ways. It is delivered under the auspices of a diversity of agencies, which includes the formal institutions of second and third-level education, as well as a variety of statutory, voluntary and community groups. The development of an effective and efficient evaluation process to ensure that quality services are accessible and responsive to the needs of young and adult alike, and that education policy and practice is designed to meet the diverse range of needs this entails, is both a challenge and a necessity. The Minister, through the Inspectorate, is charged in accordance with Paragraph 13(3)a(1) of the Education Act to evaluate the organisation and operation of recognised schools and centres, and the quality and effectiveness of the education provided in those centres.

Evaluation has a critical part to play in assisting with the development of all aspects of quality in schools and the education system. The Inspectorate has a key role in quality assurance in all areas of education, including Adult and Continuing Education.

A broad consensus is emerging within many member states of the EU that general assessments of how the system as a whole is functioning should be built on the foundation of self-assessment by schools and education centres themselves. External evaluations provide an excellent validation of the institution's own judgement. In this regard the Education Act outlines the functions of the Inspectorate to include *"to support and advise recognised schools, centres for education and teachers on matters relating to the provision of education ... "*

Ongoing programme and school/centre evaluation within Adult and Continuing Education will ensure this sector remains highly responsive, dynamic and effective in meeting the diverse and essential needs of its recipients through its many providers. It will identify best practice and inform policy and future development of this sector of education.

8.7. Research

An active and ongoing research programme is an essential ingredient in policy development and refinement in Adult Education. While a number of elements within the Adult Education sector have already well established data gathering/research capacity, this capacity is not comprehensive throughout the sector nor is it explicitly or systematically sector wide in its focus. This is a serious lacuna constraining the development of the sector. Accordingly, the National Adult Learning Council will incorporate a research role within its remit and will be provided with staff and resources for this purpose. There is a particular dearth of data on participation of specific groups in adult education, such as Travellers, students with disabilities, immigrants, processes and outcomes in Community Education, effectiveness of outreach strategies, best practice in guidance, APL and WBL etc. The research function of the National Adult Learning Council will focus in particular on these issues.

8.8 Irish Language and Culture

In many senses, there has been a major renewal of Irish cultural forms in recent years, with Irish traditional music, dance and writing through the medium of Irish flourishing within the country and attracting increasing international acclaim. Nevertheless, the promotion of Irish language and culture was highlighted in the consultation process as having been given scant attention in the Green Paper, and high levels of engagement remain to be developed between statutory and voluntary groups promoting Irish culture and those within the adult education field.

The provision and development of adult education in Irish and through Irish, both inside and outside the Gaeltacht, must be seen as an integral component of the strategy to promote adult learning in an inter-cultural and pluralist society. There has been a palpable growth of public interest and participation in Irish language courses by Irish adults wishing to learn the language and use it as a natural and normal communication in practical settings. In order to address needs in this area this Paper proposes:-

- increased and flexible provision of Irish courses and classes at locally accessible venues to cater for the needs of adults, taking account of the need to combine family, work, leisure and education roles;

- development of a structured approach leading to a graded system of assessment and certification, taking account of the work by Institiúid Teangeolaíochta na hÉireann in this area, and emerging developments under the national qualifications framework;

- providing for distance education and opportunities for self-directed learning in Irish and through Irish, supported by the appropriate materials;

- providing opportunities for staff in the adult education sector to enhance their language skills;

- enhancing the range of programmes available to adults through the medium of Irish.

White Paper on Adult Education – Learning for Life

In order to promote and co-ordinate developments in this area, an Irish Language Officer will be appointed to the National Adult Learning Council, and a sub-committee of relevant interests will be established by the Council to progress initiatives. The sub-committee will provide for participation by Irish language bodies such as Bord na Gaeilge and Comhdháil Náisiúnta na Gaeilge, adult education interests, Udarás na Gaeltachta, and representatives from VECs and Area Partnerships in Gaeltacht areas.

In Gaeltacht areas, needs have been highlighted in relation to adult literacy in the Irish language, provision of community and basic education, and ensuring an adequate range of options in the Irish language to enable participants to progress to PLC courses. Addressing the scarcity of materials and tutors, and the need to provide for different dialects in the Gaeltacht areas are part of the challenge.

In order to address these needs, the Department of Education and Science has agreed to fund a 3-year initiative in Gaeltacht areas which will be implemented jointly by VECs and the Local Area Partnerships. The objective is to develop an integrated adult basic education programme in each area through the medium of Irish, incorporating communications, literacy, language, numeracy, ICT skills and key "learning to learn" skills. Development Workers are being employed to work as an integrated team under the project, one for each dialect region. Their role is to design tutor training courses in adult basic education, to develop appropriate teaching materials and to plan and resource promotional strategies in each area, so that a basic education service through the Irish language can then be delivered locally.

8.9 Childcare

The Department of Justice, Equality and Law Reform is charged with overall responsibility for co-ordinating childcare service delivery arrangements. A major expansion will be provided in this area under a £250m programme in the National Development Plan over the period 2000-2006. This will provide for:-

- capital grants for community-based childcare services;

- grants towards staff costs for community based childcare services;

- supports to enhance the role of national voluntary childcare organisations;

Wicklow County Council
County Library Services

- flexible measures to promote facilities for children with special needs, and services in disadvantaged areas;

- a new capital grant scheme for independent childcare providers.

This will be complemented by targeted early education funding for pupils with special needs in the education sector, and by investment in the development of homework clubs in disadvantaged areas. The Department of Social Community and Family Affairs will also provide support for the development of out-of-school hours, care services by community groups.

A synergy group and a National Childcare Co-ordinating Committee have been established to ensure a co-ordinated approach at national level, and local childcare networks and County Childcare Committees are being set up to ensure integration and cohesion at local level.

In 1998, the Department of Education and Science introduced a scheme to support childcare for participants on VTOS, Youthreach and Senior Traveller Training programmes. Funds are allocated to the VECs for:-

- direct provision of crèche facilities in centres, or in rented premises, including staff, equipment/refurbishment, rental, insurance and other overheads;

- purchase of places on existing community or commercial crèches, (with priority support to the former in all cases where this is feasible). This is subject to payment of a maximum of £50 per week per child for a full-day session, with pro-rata adjustments for sessions of lesser duration;

- payment of childminders, subject to a maximum of £50 per child per week for a full session with pro-rata adjustments for part-time sessions. This is subject to compliance with tax and registration requirements under the Childcare Act.

Some 795 participants (997children) are currently benefiting from the measure. While the childminder provision was designed to be flexible to situations, particularly in rural areas, where economies of scale would not exist to justify provision of creches, the take-up in this area has been disappointing, and feedback indicates a shortage of available childminders and a fear of transferring from the black economy. In addition, rapidly rising childcare and building costs, growth in other employment opportunities, and a reduction in provision nationally of childminding places has added to difficulties in progressing the measure. Solutions to these issues are being explored in consultation with providers and the Department of Finance.

In addition, under the PLC programme, 1,103 students are pursuing childcare courses during the 1999/2000 academic year. The NCVA Level 2 Award in Childcare is recognised as a suitable qualification for employment in the Department of Education and Science Early Start programme.

Lack of childcare was highlighted in the consultation process as a critical barrier to access to education and training for adults, particularly women. Additional funds will be provided under the National Development Plan to consolidate developments to date, and to expand provision in this area on a phased basis.

8.10 Older People

OECD data on educational levels within the adult population show the high proportion of adults in the older age groups who had not had the opportunity to access education beyond the primary level. The International Adult Literacy Survey also showed a significantly higher proportion of adults in the older age group as scoring at the bottom literacy level.

Strategies for active ageing stress the critical importance of access to learning as a key tool in coping with change, and the importance of physical, social and mental activity to general well-being. In that respect, adult education can play an important role in contributing to active ageing, promoting social integration, reducing health costs, enhancing the quality of life, and providing training in new technology for many whose mobility and access to information and communication might otherwise be restricted.

Older adults have key potential within adult education as:-

- providers;
- mentors;
- literacy volunteers;
- promoters of solidarity between the ages;
- childminders;
- learners.

The Consultation Process highlighted the barriers for this group in accessing education and training through the use of criteria which are labour-market focused, and highlighted, in particular, the importance of ICT training as an aid to mobility and communication, particularly in remote rural areas.

As the general population ages, or is affected by a drift of young people out of rural areas, an increasing proportion of adults find themselves housebound with the responsibility of caring for elderly relatives. This is emerging as a barrier to access to education and training opportunities, which could become as significant a problem in years to come as the lack of childcare. It is beyond the scope of the education sector to provide services in this area. However, as part of an integrated area-based approach, the Local Adult Learning Boards will be asked to explore with the Health Boards the feasibility of strategic partnerships to co-ordinate services where feasible. Adult Education could provide learning opportunities in relation to elder care and also in relation to post-caring work areas.

The *Second Report of the Expert Group on Future Skills (2000)* has adverted to the need for employers to focus increasingly on encouraging older workers to re-enter the labour force. It is also important that the needs of this group are considered in the implementation of a lifelong learning strategy and that unnecessary and restrictive age barriers are removed.

There are no age barriers to participation on PLC, adult literacy or third-level education programmes, and this strategy will be continued in the implementation of part-time options under the Back to Education Initiative. Chapter 4 sets out arrangements under which participants who are medical card holders, recipients of non-contributory pensions or Carer's Allowances and their dependants will be eligible for free access to the Back to Education Initiative, while Chapter 7 also extends free access to part-time third-level students in these categories.

8.11 People with Disabilities

8.11.1 Current developments

Between 1,200 - 1,500 students with physical, sensory or learning disabilities participate in third-level education. The figure for VTOS on January 2000 was 410 students. Data are not available on the representation of such groups across other areas of the education sector. No specific arrangements have been made, until recently, within Further Education to cater for this group. Within the third-level sector a special flexible fund has been established towards the cost of adaptive technology, readers, transport, interpreters, care assistance etc. This was increased to £700,000 in 1999 and will be further developed under the Third-level Access programme in the National Development Plan.

As a result of a decision by Government to integrate services for people with disabilities into mainstream provision:-

- a new National Disability Authority has been established on a statutory basis under the aegis of the Department of Justice, Equality and Law Reform which will act as a disability watchdog;

- the National Social Service Board and certain functions of the National Rehabilitation Board have been merged to form a new organisation called COMHAIRLE, which comes under the aegis of the Department of Social, Community and Family Affairs;

- the National Rehabilitation Board staff have been redeployed — to Comhairle, the Audiology Service to the health services, vocational education and training posts to FÁS, and posts from the NRB's psychology service related to school children to the National Educational Psychological Service.

FÁS will provide advice, guidance and training services in relation to vocational/employment skills training at a variety of levels. FÁS will also advise on sheltered, supported or open employments options and provide a range of grants in this area for employers and employees. This will include the Employment Support Scheme, the Workplace Equipment Adaptation Grants Scheme, Disability Awareness Training Grant, Disabled Employee Re-training Grant, Job Interview Interpreter Grant, and the Personal Reader Grant.

The Health Boards will continue to provide advice, guidance and services in relation to rehabilitative type foundation and lifeskills training which is pre-vocational in nature, and community workshops or other sheltered or supported work options.

The Health Boards and FÁS will continue to use specialist agencies to assist them. An inter-agency Establishment Group is co-ordinating the transition arrangements.

A pilot "Action for Disability" project has been in operation in FÁS since the beginning of 1998. The aim of the project is to facilitate people with disabilities to participate in all FÁS programmes. To date, 340 people have availed of the services of the project in three FÁS Regions – Dublin North, Dublin South, and the Southwest. It is hoped to draw upon the experiences of FÁS staff in these regions to help FÁS offer a quality service to people with disabilities.

FÁS is in the process of implementing the recommendations of an NRB commissioned Access Audit to ensure people with disabilities will have easy access to FÁS premises.

RECOMMENDATIONS

The transfer of responsibility for training of people with disabilities to FÁS is not intended to obviate the need for all education and training providers to make specific provision to ensure that people with disabilities can access mainstream services. A range of actions is being proposed in order to progress this area:-

- people with disabilities should be targeted by every Adult Education programme so that they may avail of integrated mainstream options on an equal basis;

- disability awareness training should be developed and provided for Adult Education and training staff generally in order to promote awareness of the barriers facing students with disabilities; to promote the cultural relevance of programmes; to encourage dialogue with disability groups and individual participants as to how programmes can be adapted to their needs; to share practice on how barriers can be overcome;

- the existing third-level fund under which additional supports (adaptive technology, readers, interpreters, care assistance and transport etc) are made available should be expanded to cover the other areas of Adult Education.

8.11.2 The operation of the existing schemes should be enhanced to ensure:-

- earlier processing of applications;

- mechanisms are provided through the fund for professional advice and assessment of individuals' needs for adaptive technology, based on the experience of the recent HORIZON projects in this area;

- that adaptive technology can be assigned to individuals, rather than institutions, so that it can be transferred from one learning sector/setting/level to another;

- arrangements to enable students to keep equipment for ongoing personal use where a period of at least 3 years usage has expired.

The existing scheme, while presently under-resourced, has been identified as having considerable potential as a model of intervention which could be developed and expanded to provide for increased integration of people with disabilities. The consultation process also highlighted the need for closer involvement of national disability interests in the development and implementation of criteria and assessment processes for the scheme.

8.11.3 The consultation process highlighted the need for flexible access routes to third-level, but for national co-ordinated standards to be developed which would protect academic standards, assess the true potential of the candidate, and operate on an equitable and transparent basis. Relevant and flexible modes of assessment, additional time for examinations, provision of access programmes, additional tuition, counselling/mentoring were also identified. The needs of participants with disabilities should be taken account of specifically in emerging developments under the National Qualifications Authority of Ireland.

8.11.4 Distance learning methodologies have particular relevance to students with disabilities, and programme content and support services should be designed with this in mind. In addition, students in receipt of a long-term disability welfare payment should have free access to relevant, nationally certified distance learning programmes in Ireland.

8.11.5 The use of Irish Sign language in Adult Education should be developed and the shortage of trained personnel in this area addressed on a phased basis. In that context a sizeable grant will be provided to the Irish Deaf Society to develop a service, over the next five years, which will address the literacy needs of deaf people throughout Ireland. Based on the experience of a successful pilot project, **Linkup**, funded under the Women's Education Initiative, 25 tutors will be trained to deliver adult literacy classes through Irish Sign Language and to give literacy courses to deaf people in five locations around Ireland. The objective is to reach as many deaf people with literacy difficulties as feasible and enable them to participate effectively in society and reduce their isolation. In addition, some of the tutors will receive further training to become facilitators, who will be able to provide trainee tutor-training nation-wide.

8.11.6 Access Officers in third-level colleges will continue to network to share practice and experience and to make policy recommendations to the Higher Education Authority on the scope for improved services.

8.11.7 All new buildings should be accessible to students with disabilities, and existing premises assessed for compliance with this need. In the provision of capital for further education, priority should be given to the adaptation of premises where needs arise.

These recommendations will be progressed on a phased basis in consultation with the relevant interests. The National Adult Learning Council will be asked to establish an Advisory Committee to report within a specific timeframe on developments in this area, and to monitor progress. An Access Officer will be appointed to the Council to co-ordinate and support the task.

As part of the development of performance indicators for the system, tracking mechanisms should be developed to monitor the participation of students with disabilities at every level of the system.

8.12 Travellers

While it is known that almost 900 travellers participate on Youthreach and Senior Traveller Training Centre programmes, there are no data on their participation levels elsewhere within the further and third-level system. A similar need arises to ensure specific strategies for integration into mainstream options - awareness training, culturally relevant programmes and materials, an inter-cultural anti-racist curriculum, supporting services such as guidance and childcare, and outreach networking and dialogue with Traveller organisations and individuals concerning the delivery of programmes. The need for specific data to support benchmarking and monitoring of progress arises.

Catering for cultural diversity needs to be a concern in all spheres of provision. In particular, there is a need for Traveller women and men to be targeted within adult literacy and VTOS programmes and for dialogue on how the schemes can be adapted to strengthen their relevance for these groups. The employment of Travellers within these services need to be encouraged given their importance as role models in the community.

In line with the recommendations made by the Inter-Departmental Group on Literacy for the Unemployed, a review of financial barriers to participation in education and training is needed. These include the removal of anomalies in regard to secondary benefits and the treatment of income disregards where both spouses have a training allowance or welfare payment.

8.13 Refugees and Asylum Seekers

8.13.1 Refugees are entitled to the same access to education and training as Irish nationals. Within the first and second-level systems, which are catering for increasing numbers of children who are immigrants, refugees or asylum seekers, arrangements have recently been introduced to provide additional teaching resources in schools with large numbers of children for whom English is not the mother tongue. In relation to adults, a Refugee Language Support Unit has been established in Trinity College to co-ordinate language assessment and tuition on a national basis. However, at present asylum seekers are not in a position to access any services of this nature. This poses particular difficulties for parents and siblings of children who are trying to integrate into Irish schools, and causes problems for schools in promoting home/school links.

A Government decision has allowed asylum seekers who entered the country before 26 July 1999 and who have been waiting at least a year for a determination of status to be given a work permit. There are an estimated 1,700 - 4,000 in this category, 75% of whom are over 18 (as more time elapses the number who have been here a year will increase, until the ceiling is reached on 26 July 2000). This also enables them to switch from Health Board Assistance to Unemployment Benefit/Assistance, and should, therefore, confer access to active labour market programmes of education and training –e.g. VTOS (if over 21 and at least 6 months on unemployment benefit or assistance) FÁS etc.

In principle, the Government is anxious to expand the role of the Refugee Language Support Unit to include provision for asylum seekers, and to explore the scope for providing a national programme in this area through the VECs and other further education providers. As a first step, a study will be undertaken to assess the likely numbers who may need additional language assistance, and discussions will be held with the relevant Departments and agencies to assess the implications of this in terms of funding and co-ordination staff, and implementation arrangements.

8.13.2 This Paper proposes the following policy in relation to the participation in education and training of asylum seekers:-

- **children aged between 15-**

    - referral to school or Youthreach, as appropriate;

- **for asylum seekers *with* entitlement to work** (all pre-26 July 1999 asylum seekers who are at least one year in Ireland):-

    - free access to adult literacy, English language and mother culture supports;

    - free access to active labour market programmes such as VTOS or PLC if over 21 and six months registered unemployed, on the same basis as other participants. As non-EU nationals they would not get maintenance grants for full-time PLC courses, but no fees would be charged, given the fact that there has never been a State fee for PLCs;

    - access to free part-time Back to Education Initiative programmes up to and including PLC level for social welfare recipients, under arrangements set out for Category 2 in Chapter 4;

Access to education and training programmes will be allowed for this group on the clear understanding that enrolment is without prejudice to the determination reached on their asylum status, and cannot be used as a basis for seeking an extension or remaining in the State should their application for asylum be rejected.

In line with other non-EU nationals, access to third-level education will apply only on payment of the economic fee, and there will be no entitlement to maintenance grants.

- **for those who do *not* have an entitlement to work;**

    - free access to adult literacy, English language and mother culture supports.

8.14 Rural Development

The Adult Education and training sector has an important role to play in promoting and sustaining development in rural communities. This will be progressed through:-

- an active role in the implementation of the National Spatial Strategy as it emerges;

- working closely with Teagasc and other agencies in supporting training for off-farm income generation under the Rural Viability Programme, particularly in the areas of enterprise, literacy, ICT training, tourism, teleworking;

- supporting and promoting the cultural identity of rural areas;

- optimising the use of the existing network of schools for Adult Education activity;

- supporting the continued viability of rural schools;

- exploring innovatory approaches to addressing transport barriers, including distance learning, mobile outreach facilities and co-operation with Area-Based Partnerships and local authorities in transport sharing schemes;

- participation in the National Rural Development Forum;

- rural proofing of policies and practice on an ongoing basis;

- promoting integrated area-based approaches through the work of the Local Adult Learning Boards and the County Development Boards.

8.15 Homeless

In an overall hierarchy of needs, homeless people are unlikely to prioritise access to education and training over more fundamental needs for food and shelter, emotional stability and help with addiction, health or welfare problems. Therefore an integrated approach is needed where accommodation, welfare and health needs are addressed as a priority, supported by opportunities to access further learning.

The Government Strategy on Homelessness provides for the establishment of a homeless services centre, within the Dublin area, to manage and co-ordinate the delivery of integrated services for the homeless in the Dublin area by statutory and voluntary agencies to address the accommodation, health, education, training, employment, personal and social needs. The service will have dedicated staff located in the centre from Dublin Corporation and the Eastern Health Authority together with a co-ordinator from FÁS and the VEC with appropriate linkages with the Probation Service.

The work of the education co-ordinator will focus on the development of outreach links with relevant statutory and community and voluntary groups, reporting on learning needs for homeless people and co-ordinating the provision of appropriate literacy, community or basic education programmes in line with the needs identified. Provision will embrace a spectrum ranging from initial tuition and guidance located in hostels to specific programmes for the homeless in education and training centres, and progression from there to mainstream learning options. Provision of back-up welfare, health and guidance and counselling services have been identified as a critical pre-requisite if the approach is to be effective.

8.16 Prisoners and Ex-Offenders

The Prison Education Service incorporates important partnership between the Department of Justice Equality and Law Reform, the VECs, the Open University, the Arts Council, several third-level colleges and a range of other bodies. Over 250 VEC staff (179 whole-time equivalents) are currently allocated to the prisons through 10 VECs on the basis of recommendations from the Department of Justice, Equality and Law Reform. This number is due to increase to about 200 whole-time equivalent staff from 2000/01. The estimated cost of the service is approximately £5m annually.

Research has consistently shown that offenders generally come from the most marginalised groups in society and typically are at high risk being unemployed, unqualified, addicted, experiencing multiple disadvantage and finding it exceptionally difficult to re-integrate into the labour market.

Under the National Development Plan 2000-2006, £70.7m is being invested in provision of work experience, vocational training and personal supports to custodial prisoners and offenders and their families in order to help them to successfully re-integrate into the social and economic life of their communities.

A key priority for the education sector in this context will be to enhance the relevance and diversity of provision within the prison education service and to strengthen the linkages between in-prison provision and that available for prisoners on release, in collaboration with other relevant agencies. The Bridge Project which is provided through a collaboration of FÁS, VEC and the Probation Service, and the Dillon's Cross Project in Cork City working with prisoners' families will provide important models for future action in this area.

8.17 Conclusion

The Government recognises that there are fundamental foundation blocks which must be put in place in building a comprehensive system of Adult Education within an overall framework of lifelong learning. In particular these include expanded provision for Training of Trainers, an inter-agency Working Group to make recommendations on the recognition of qualifications for adult education practitioners; a Forum of Adult Education Practitioners; new approaches to assessment, accreditation and certification through the work of the of the National Qualifications Authority of Ireland and development of an Educational Adult Guidance and Counselling service.

This Chapter also sets out arrangements for research and quality assurance, and for the development of other supporting services such as childcare. In addition, provision for increased access to mainstream adult education programmes for people with disabilities, travellers, refugees and asylum seekers, the homeless, and prisoners and ex-offenders, and to address barriers in rural areas are key features of the development of an equality strategy within the adult education sector.

Chapter 9
Co-Operation with Northern Ireland

CHAPTER 9
Co-Operation with Northern Ireland

9.1 Many of the concerns and issues highlighted in this Paper are also the focal point of strategies in other countries to promote a framework of lifelong learning as a central part of policies to maintain growth, employment, competitiveness, social inclusion and citizenship.

9.2 White Paper: *A New Learning Culture for All*

9.2.1 In Northern Ireland, following consultations on a Green Paper *The Learning Age 1998*, the Government set out its policies for development of the Adult Education and training sector in a paper entitled *Lifelong Learning: A New Learning Culture for All (1999)*, published by the Department of Education, Northern Ireland and the Training and Employment Agency.

The aims of the strategy outlined in the Paper are to:-

- *"increase significantly adult participation in vocational education and training, including access to further and higher education and training from groups previously under-represented;*

- *emphasise the development of key and basic skills;*

- *ensure greater progression through the system of qualifications;*

- *provide for a more coherent relationship between education and training provision and the skill needs of the regional economy;*

- *enhance collaboration between education and training providers and the world of business and industry;*

- *enhance significantly the information and communications (ICT) skills of teachers, instructors and students;*

- *sustain and improve the quality of provision and enhance the performance across the education and training sectors."*

9.2.2 The Paper highlighted:-

- a 76% participation rate in full-time education of 16-17 year olds;

- 40% of the unemployed and 19% of the employed had no qualifications *(1998 Labour Force Spring Survey);*

- 24% of adults in Northern Ireland scored at the bottom literacy level in the International OECD Adult Literacy Survey;

- low participation rates in formal learning by adults at 28% compared with 40% in England *(Gallup Poll 1996).*

9.2.3 The White Paper sets out an action plan for change and development to be achieved over the period 1999-2002, which includes:-

- a major expansion of provision including 30,000 education, training or work/community experience places under a New Deal programme for the unemployed, 2,000 extra full-time equivalent places in higher education, and expansion in further education by 8,000 full-time and part-time places;

- increased partnerships between further education colleges and local business interests, trade unions, other education providers, community and voluntary sector interests, to encourage adults to return to learning and to co-ordinate activity to meet local needs;

- the establishment of a comprehensive skills monitoring unit for monitoring skills shortages and recruitment difficulties and forecasting skills needs, in order to inform the planning and delivery of vocational education and training. This will complement the work of the Northern Ireland Skills Taskforce;

- the creation of 25,000 Individual Learning Accounts supported by Government to the value of £150 each to encourage individuals and employers to invest in their own learning. As part of this, Career Development Loans (deferred repayment bank loans guaranteed by the Department in partnership with banks, and Career Development Accounts (enabling learners to save and borrow towards learning and allowing employers to invest) are being tested.

- the establishment of a University for Industry (UFL) to promote and market education and training and facilitate increased access and choice. This will provide a free phone "Learning Direct" information and guidance service, progressively develop referral to local guidance services, provide for course registration services for learners to electronically linked UFL courses, and pilot arrangements for linking to individual learning accounts, and a personal learning record. Schools, libraries, further and higher education colleges, and community providers will be connected electronically to a National Grid for Learning. The process also includes investment in ICT training for staff in the sector, enhancement of network infrastructure linking education centres, and supporting ICT based curriculum development;

- the establishment of a Basic Skills Unit to raise standards in literacy, numeracy and basic IT in partnership with providers, social partners and community and voluntary sector interests. The unit will fulfil an advisory and advocacy role, promoting awareness, sharing good practice, supporting practitioners, providing quality resources and materials, and funding community groups for activities in basic Adult Education. It will also develop close links with the media to encourage the development of appropriate radio and television programmes;

- commitment to the development of a national framework for qualifications and the Northern Ireland Credit Accumulation and Transfer System to promote access and progression up and across academic, vocational and occupational routes.

9.3 National Development Plan

It is clear that there are extensive opportunities to co-operate and share experience in areas of mutual concern. Both the National Development Plan for Ireland and the Development Plan for Northern Ireland include a common chapter on cross border co-operation. This has 3 dimensions - co-operation along the border corridor and between Northern Ireland and the border counties in the South; North/South co-operation within the overall island; and East-West co-operation between Ireland, Great Britain, Europe and internationally. Key concerns overall are to increase competitiveness; to address infrastructural issues in the communications and electronic commerce sector; to promote development of inland waterways, marine tourism, aquaculture, agriculture and tourism.

Within the education and training sector there will be a particular focus on joint co-operation in:-

- inter-active approaches at university and further education level in such areas as R&D and support for small and medium sized enterprises;

- the development of lifelong learning, adult literacy and adult guidance and counselling programmes, and promotion education/community/business links;

- information and communications technology in schools;

- addressing educational under-achievement.

Under the Special EU Support Programme for Peace and Reconciliation, a Centre for Cross-Border Studies, based in Armagh, has been established to research and develop co-operation across the border areas in education, business, public administration and communications. The Centre is undertaking research in collaboration with the relevant Departments, North and South, in relation to the scale and impact of cross-border exchange programmes.

9.4 North/South Ministerial Council

Within the context of the North/South Ministerial Council for Education established under the Good Friday Agreement, particular priority is being given to joint co-operation in:-

- addressing special education needs and educational under-achievement;

- promoting teacher mobility;

- mutual recognition of qualifications;

- school, youth and teacher exchanges.

9.5 Other Areas for Co-Operation

Other areas targeted for joint co-operation include:-

- sharing practice under the National Anti-Poverty Strategy and the Targeting Social Need initiative in Northern Ireland;

- promoting reconciliation, building local capacity and promoting the inclusion of marginalised groups;

- addressing labour shortages and promoting lifelong learning;

9.6 A new Institute for British/Irish Studies has been established at UCD to promote and conduct research in the area of the Northern Ireland conflict, and North/South and East/West relations. Formal links have been established between the Institute and universities in London, Edinburgh, Cardiff and Belfast. This will have a major impact on research in the social sciences, and will complement the massively increased investment in research generally within the third-level sector. The research that the Institute undertakes has the potential to make a valuable contribution to the political process to achieve peace and prosperity.

9.7 This work will be progressed and strengthened in the years ahead through the development of strategic links at national and local levels between North/South education and training providers and policy makers. The work will be supported through the appointment of a staff member in the National Adult Learning Council for this purpose, and who will also focus on the potential of best international practice which can inform future policies and strategies in the field of Adult Education and training.

Chapter 10
Structures

CHAPTER 10
Structures

10.1 The challenge of coming up with an Adult Education structure is one of creating a framework for the sector which accords it a higher level of priority in mainstream provision while ensuring innovation, flexibility, responsiveness and learner-centred commitment. The Green Paper stressed the need for such a structure to:-

- seek integration while celebrating diversity and innovation;

- be locally responsive within a national framework of objectives;

- focus on Adult Education with reference to lifelong learning objectives;

- model ways of decision-making that include the participant and the provider;

- seek complementarity rather than uniformity;

- ensure a focus on targeted and effective programmes.

The challenge is to provide a structure that can provide a co-ordinating and formalising framework while preserving the innate creativity, expansiveness and user-driven principles that underpin quality in the sector. The lifelong and lifewide dimension of the Adult Education agenda implies an intimidating diversity of providers with associated differences in ideologies, methodologies, outcomes and constituencies. It is clearly imperative that this multiple sourced provision is integrated and co-ordinated. The institutional challenges of such co-ordination are immense, and demand that there is parity of esteem between the different stakeholders if the sector is to be promoted and developed effectively.

The Green Paper identified the following stakeholders in the Adult Education sector:

- Participants/Learners;
- Providers;
- Funders;
- Social Partners;
- Accrediting Bodies;
- Practitioners;
- Policy Makers.

It noted the importance of involving each of the stakeholders in comprehensive and inclusionary structures for Adult Education at national and local level.

10.2 National Adult Learning Council (NALC)

10.2.1 The Green Paper noted that despite a number of *Reports (Murphy 1973; Kenny 1984)* recommending the establishment of a national statutory body with responsibility for Adult Education, little progress had been made in establishing such a body.

This is a serious omission that now needs to be addressed as a priority. The Government, therefore, now proposes to proceed with the establishment by the Minister for Education and Science, of a National Adult Learning Council as an Executive Agency of the Department under the statutory framework of the Education Act 1998.

10.2.2 Terms of Reference

The terms of reference of the National Adult Learning Council will be as outlined in the Green Paper, namely:-

- to promote the development of the Adult Education sector in line with national social and economic needs;

- to promote co-ordination of the work of participating bodies within an agreed national strategy and policy framework, and to liaise with the wide variety of stakeholders in the field;

- to advise on Adult Education priorities;

- to monitor the implementation of an agreed strategy;

- to advise Government on policy and related matters in the field of Adult Education;

- to liaise with the other education sectors in facilitating the achievement of lifelong learning objectives;

- to fund, co-ordinate and monitor the delivery of programme and staff development initiatives for designated Adult Education programmes within the Further Education sector of the Department of Education and Science;

- to advise on quality standards in Adult Education provision in consultation with the National Qualifications Authority of Ireland, and to facilitate the dissemination of good practice;

- to engage in research and evaluation in the field of Adult Education;

- to promote cross border and international co-operation in Adult Education.

The terms of reference outlined above concentrate the work of the NALC on the critical areas of co-ordination, liaison, policy advice, monitoring, quality, staff development and research. As constituted at present, they do not envisage a function for the Council as a funding and administration body in relation to programmes (other than staff development programmes) in the Further Education sector. However, this issue will be re-visited in the light of emerging developments in relation to a review of organisational structures and roles within the Department of Education and Science itself. For some time, the need has been recognised for the Department to divest itself of a range of administrative tasks to intermediary bodies or executive agencies in order to enable it to concentrate more effectively on its strategic role.

10.2.3 Structure

The NALC will have a Governing Board, the membership of which will be composed of:-

- one representative nominated by Aontas;

- one representative nominated by the National Adult Literacy Agency;

- two representatives nominated by the community and voluntary pillar;

- one representative from each of the training agencies FÁS, Teagasc and CERT;

- one representative from the each of the following management bodies - Irish Vocational Education Association; Joint Management Body and

Association of Community and Comprehensive Schools;

- one representative each from the Teachers' Union of Ireland and the Association of Secondary Teachers of Ireland;

- one representative nominated by the Union of Students of Ireland;

- two representatives from employers;

- one representative nominated by ICTU;

- one representative nominated by the Higher Education Authority;

- one representative nominated by the Council of Directors of Institutes of Technology;

- one representative nominated by the Council of Heads of Irish Universities;

- one representative of the National Qualifications Authority of Ireland;

- two nominees of the Minister for Education and Science;

- two nominees of the Minister for Enterprise, Trade and Employment.

The Chairperson of the Council will be appointed by the Minister for Education and Science in consultation with the Minister for Enterprise, Trade and Employment.

10.2.4 The Council staff structure will have four broad units within it as follows:-

- Adult Education and the Formal Education Sector;

- Workplace Learning;

- Community Education;

- Research.

The terms of reference for each of these Units will be as set out below.

Adult Education and the Formal Education Sector

The role of the Adult Education and the Formal Education Sector Unit will be:-

- to support Adult Education providers and the work of the Local Adult Learning Boards in terms of area planning, curriculum development, programme delivery and evaluation, and integration of provision;

- to co-ordinate and provide an appropriate staff development programme for the Further Education sector;

- to promote and co-ordinate support services for adult learners, e.g. a guidance service;

- to promote and facilitate broadly based interaction amongst the key stakeholders in Adult Education;

- to advise on policy and quality assurance;

- to support Higher Education institutions in expanding their mature student provision;

- to promote the development of appropriate Adult Education services through Irish to meet the needs of Gaeltacht and non-Gaeltacht regions;

- to promote equality of participation, benefit and outcome from Adult Education for participants from under-represented groups, particularly people with disabilities, and travellers, and to monitor progress in this area.

It is intended that this Unit will have a key role in co-ordinating and supporting the work of the national co-ordinators already in place across the Further Education system for Youthreach, VTOS, Senior Traveller Training Centres and Adult Literacy, but that the personnel concerned will continue to be sited in their present locations. In effect, the National Adult Learning Council will integrate the work of the Further Education Support Service referred to in the Green Paper into its framework of activities, but will ensure continued flexibility in the dispersal of such staff, as appropriate, in locations throughout the country.

An Access Officer will be engaged to promote and develop and support the implementation of an equality strategy for participation of Travellers and those with disabilities in Adult Education. The Unit will also establish the Advisory Committee referred to in Chapter 8 to report within a specific timeframe on developments in the integration of people with physical and learning disabilities into Adult Education, and to monitor progress in this area.

An Irish Language Officer will work within the Unit to promote the development of Adult Education in Irish and through Irish, to liaise with national level Irish language bodies, and to co-ordinate the development of initiatives in this area. The Council will establish a sub-committee to promote and monitor developments, which will provide for representation from bodies such as Bord na Gaeilge, Comhdháil Náisiúnta na Gaeilge, Údaras na Gaeltachta, adult education interests and VECs and Area-Based Partnerships from Gaeltacht areas.

Workplace Learning

The role of the Workplace Learning Unit will be:-

- to support the establishment of education/training/workplace consortia through the work of the Local Adult Learning Boards;

- to promote innovative approaches to workplace learning, particularly in the application of ICT and distance education;

- to explore with the National Qualifications Authority of Ireland the feasibility of establishing a panel of Learning Assessors and Designated Assessment Centres for purposes of APL and WBL, and to support the quality of provision in this area;

- to promote opportunities for poorly qualified labour market entrants to continue to upgrade their skills;

- to promote the capacity of the Adult Education system to address skills needs in the workplace, particularly in relation to new technology, foreign languages and areas where shortages have been highlighted by the Expert Group on Future Skill Needs.

Community Education

The role of the Community Education Unit will be:-

- to promote, co-ordinate and network the work of the Community Education Facilitators;

- to promote the role of Community Education groups as providers of Adult Education;

- to interact with the NGO structure throughout the country in developing a Community Education model in a number of sectors, namely:-

  - Community-Based Women's Groups;
  - Men's Groups;
  - Travellers and other Ethnic Minorities;
  - People with Disabilities;
  - Community Arts Groups;
  - Older People;

- to promote and monitor innovative pedagogical approaches in community education;

- to promote in association with the National Qualifications Authority of Ireland the development of appropriate mechanisms for the assessment and accreditation of community learning;

- promote the development of partnerships between statutory agencies and community education groups;

- to promote equality of participation, benefit and outcome from Adult Education for participants from under-represented groups, particularly people with disabilities, and Travellers, and to monitor progress in this area;

White Paper on Adult Education – Learning for Life

- to identify and share good practice particularly in the areas of outreach, access and participation of marginalised groups in Adult Education.

Research

The role of the Research Unit will be:-

- to undertake or commission research, studies, evaluations and/or data gathering on participation and provision in Adult Education which will:-

  - inform the development of policy initiatives targeted on areas of need;

  - track the participation of minorities and other disadvantaged groups within the commitment to equality and multiculturalism;

  - identify and document models of best practice in all aspects of adult and lifelong learning;

  - maintain an awareness of Ireland's position with regard to adult learning within an international context.

- to advise on the development of performance indicators which should be used to monitor the quality and effectiveness of provision;

- to undertake and evaluate on a rolling basis all aspects of Adult Education provision and to liaise with the Inspectorate in this area;

- to promote and develop strategic linkages with Adult Education providers overseas, particularly in relation to North/South, East/West and EU relations.

10.2.5 There are limitations as to the representation that can be provided for within the structures of the National Adult Learning Council. Therefore, part of the work of the Council will be to establish and convene appropriate fora through which wider representation can influence policy and practice. This approach should provide for the Forum for Practitioners in Adult Education mentioned in Chapter 8, as well as providing a vehicle for a stronger role for groups representing Disability, Traveller and community education interests. It also provides a mechanism to forge strategic links with organisations such as the Arts Council, An Chomhairle Leabharlanna and the Library Service, the National Centre for Guidance in Education,   Area

Development Management, the Prison Education Service, Udaras na Gaeltachta, professional bodies, County/City Development Boards, Access Officers in third-level colleges, the National Adult Literacy Agency etc who have a key role to play in the delivery of an effective Adult Education service. Links with the Youth Service, with Youthreach, the National Council for Curriculum and Assessment, the Home/School/Liaison service, Probation and Welfare Services and employment services, and the work of the Educational Welfare Board are also a vital part of the approach.

10.2.6 Staff

The National Adult Learning Council will have a core management staff of six - a Chief Executive, a Finance/Personnel/ IT Officer, and four Unit Heads, responsible for each of the Units outlined above. It will also have an Access Officer, an Irish Language Officer and a Research/International Officer, be supported with the necessary technical and administrative staff, and be in a position to draw on the resources elsewhere within the system, such as national co-ordinators, Adult Education organisers, community education facilitators etc.

10.3 Local Adult Learning Boards (LALBs)

10.3.1 The task of putting in place structures for the planning, management and development of Adult and Community Education provision at local level involves a recognition that provision is currently fragmented, lacks a strategic area-based approach and is under-resourced; and that the ad hoc Adult Education Boards have not been successful in addressing needs.

There is widespread agreement with the view propounded in the Green Paper that:-

> *"Effective local structures for co-ordination of Adult Education should recognise the need for a multiplicity of providers and allow statutory and voluntary providers to work in harmony and partnership to meet local needs".*

10.3.2 Terms of Reference

Thirty-three Local Adult Education Boards will be established throughout the country to:-

- establish the level of Adult Education needs in their region;

- develop an integrated action plan at local level to meet these needs, ensuring full complementarity with training and education services provided by other bodies;

- promote and develop a comprehensive information service regarding the full range of services available locally;

- promote the co-ordination and complementarity of developments in regard to the Employment Services and the evolution of the Adult Educational Guidance Service;

- be responsible for the co-ordination of the work of participating bodies at local level;

- facilitate the targeting of Adult Education resources on area priorities in the context of an agreed lifelong learning strategy;

- to promote equality of participation, benefit and outcome from Adult Education for participants from under-represented groups, particularly people with disabilities, and travellers, and monitor progress in this area;

- decide on the deployment of Adult Education resources within the education sector on the basis of agreed national criteria;

- promote and support the development of Community Education provision, and the development of partnerships between the community and voluntary and statutory sectors;

- provide organisational, administrative, professional and financial support to Adult Education services in the area;

- report annually to the National Adult Learning Council on the delivery of services in the region.

Members of the boards would be chosen for their expertise and involvement in the field of Adult Education and training, their knowledge of area needs and their capacity to influence and report on decision-making and delivery in their respective agencies.

10.3.3 Structure

Membership of the Local Adult Learning Boards should include:-

- four representatives nominated by the community and voluntary pillar, including Travellers and disability interests;

- one representative from each of the training agencies, FÁS, Teagasc and CERT;

- one representative nominated by each of the school sectors in the area – vocational, secondary, and community/comprehensive;

- one representative each from the Teachers' Union of Ireland and the Association of Secondary Teachers of Ireland;

- one representative of learners;

- two representatives from employers;

- one representative nominated by ICTU;

- one representative of the Area Partnership;

- two representatives of the VEC;

- one representative of the County/City Development Board;

- one representative of the Library Service;

- one representative from the adult literacy service;

- one representative of the health boards;

- one representative of the Institutes of Technology, where there is such provision in the Board's catchment area;

- 1 representative of the university sector where there is such provision in the Board's catchment area.

10.3.4 Establishing and Hosting the Boards

The Local Adult Learning Boards will be established within the provisions of Section 21 of the Vocational Education Act (1930), as statutory sub-committees of the VEC. This will require that the amending VEC legislation currently being processed should abolish the existing restraints that limit the size of a sub-committee to 12. Under Section 21(5) of the 1930 Act, the Minister will approve arrangements for the VECs to dispense with the requirements under which all acts of the Local Adult Learning Boards require the confirmation of the VEC committee. This will enable the

Local Adult Learning Boards to act as autonomous sub-committees which are administratively hosted by the VEC, and where the VEC also provides a technical service as an employer of additional staff appointed to the Boards. The Boards will have authority to make decisions on the deployment of resources within each region in regard to designated programmes within the further education sector accordance with:-

- the national standards prescribed by the National Qualifications Authority of Ireland;

- the standards and guidelines for good practice and the national policies prescribed by the National Adult Learning Council;

- the framework for accountability, provision, policy, quality and resources set out by the Department of Education and Science.

10.3.5 The principles that should underpin the operation of the Boards will be as set out in the Green Paper: -

- Area-based planning;

- Social Inclusion and Community Development;

- Access, Quality, Relevance and Progression;

- Partnership;

- Integration;

- Information;

- Flexibility;

- Voluntary effort;

- Devolved authority.

In addition, Local Adult Learning Boards will be required to ensure parity of esteem between the different interest groups, and that each member of the Board has full and equal status. The area Education Officers/Adult Education Officers will be ex-officio members of the Local Adult Learning Boards. The Chief Executive Officer of the VEC may attend ex-officio any meeting of the Local Adult Learning Board. The remit of the CEO as Accounting Officer will extend to the work of the Local Adult Learning Boards.

10.3.6 The term of office of the Boards will be 3 years' duration or such periods as may be co-terminous with the life of the VEC. The Boards will be required to meet at least 4 times per year, and will convene extraordinary meetings when the need arises.

The Members of the Board shall, at their first meeting, elect one of their members as Chairperson.

The quorum shall be 8 members.

A special meeting of the Board may be convened by any 10 members.

10.3.7 Community Fora

It is essential that democratic and accountable processes are put in place to enable the full range of local providers to play a role in the development of area plans and to inform ongoing policy and practice in Adult Education. Therefore, the **Local Adult Learning Boards will be required to formally convene local community fora through which the views of a wide range of interest can be channelled.** The fora should be convened by way of public meetings to which all interest groups with a role in Adult Education should be invited. This should include schools, Community and Adult Education groups, youth, adult literacy, welfare, health, employment centres, and training agencies. Appropriate networks should also be established where necessary through which:-

- nominations can be made for membership of the Local Adult Learning Boards;

- the needs of specific groups such as Travellers and people with disabilities can be progressed.

10.3.8 Funding

It is envisaged that **existing services** which are currently the remit of the VEC, or of individual schools, will continue to be funded on that basis into the future, but that the Local Adult Learning Boards, will, when they are established, have a key role in determining the priorities for:-

- deployment of funds under the Community Education budget;

- allocation of resources under the Special Initiatives for Disadvantaged Adults Scheme;

- determination of priorities for expansion of places under the Back to Education Initiative;

- overseeing of the Adult Educational guidance service as it emerges.

Funding will be allocated to the **relevant providers** on the basis of an annual area plan submitted by the Board to the Department of Education and Science e.g. staff/funds will be allocated to individual schools or VECs in line with existing practice, and in the case of over-arching services such as guidance, staff development, SPIDAS, community education, funds will be allocated to the VECs on a technical basis for deployment locally in accordance with the recommendations of the Local Adult Learning Boards. The VECs will provide accounting and technical services to the Local Adult Learning Boards.

10.3.9 Local Adult Learning Boards will be required to submit an annual report for each year ended 31 December, and provide a copy to the VEC, a copy to the National Adult Learning Council and a copy to the Department of Education and Science. This should document the overall provision by programme in the area, provide a profile of participants, and report on the key developments. In addition, expenditure of the Board should be included under a separate heading in the monthly returns of expenditure made by the VEC to the Department on an ongoing basis. The Local Adult Learning Boards will also co-ordinate the provision of performance indicators on a quarterly basis on the delivery of services in their areas.

The VECs will be allocated funds to support the networking and operational costs of the Local Adult Learning Boards.

10.4 Adult Education Organisers

The Adult Education Organisers (AEOs) were first appointed in 1979. Although attached to the VECs, their terms of reference included a role with non-VEC providers also.

Since their appointment, the AEOs have been central to the development of Adult Education in Ireland. Apart from supporting and co-ordinating the night-class provision of schools, they have played a pivotal role in the emergence of the Adult Literacy movement; in the development and implementation of new second-chance initiatives such as Youthreach and VTOS; in supporting Community Education initiatives and in the emerging policy debate.

Currently there are 43 Adult Education Organisers throughout the country. The Government now proposes to appoint a further 35 in the context of the additional work arising from the planned expansion of provision, the role of the Local Adult Learning Boards, and of promoting an increased role for community and comprehensive and secondary school sectors in providing for adult learning. Of these, 33 will be appointed to the Local Adult Learning Boards on a flexible needs basis, to be deployed in accordance with the priorities identified by the Boards. At local level, there will be a particular need to convene local networks of secondary and C&C schools, to promote, support and develop their role in adult education provision, and develop good linkages with the other stakeholders and providers in the area. Arrangements for nomination of representatives from the secondary and the community and comprehensive schools sector onto Local Adult Learning Boards will also stem from this process.

Two of the additional Adult Education Organisers will be assigned to the National Adult Learning Council. A particular part of their remit will be to play a national co-ordinating role in networking community, comprehensive and secondary schools and in ensuring a democratic and streamlined framework for representation of these sectors in the work of the Local Adult Learning Boards, and that of Council. Networking in national fora, co-ordination of policy inputs and responses in the field of Adult Education, promoting and supporting an increased role for these sectors in adult learning, organisation of appropriate staff development programmes, and close collaboration with the relevant management bodies will be an important part of this process. The national co-ordinators will report to the National Adult Learning Council, and their priorities and work programme will be agreed jointly by the Department and the Council in discussion with the relevant management bodies.

A key function of the local AEOs will be to support and develop the role of schools as providers of Adult Education, and to work closely with other community interests to ensure an integrated approach in the delivery of Adult Education and training. Such interests will include VECs, FÁS, Area Partnerships, libraries, youth, community and voluntary sector groups, employers, County/City Development Boards, health and welfare interests and employment services. They will also be asked to work explicitly with the County Library system towards enabling the realisation of the vast potential of this system as a vehicle for accessible learning opportunities countrywide. The key objective is to co-ordinate the work of education providers with their counterparts in the other sectors in promoting an integrated area-based approach to the development and implementation of an Adult Education plan within their geographic areas.

The operation of the Local Adult Learning Boards will be evaluated after a 3-year development phase to assess its effectiveness and make recommendations as to how an integrated strategy can best be enhanced for the future development of the sector.

White Paper on Adult Education – Learning for Life

10.5 County/City Development Boards

The Local Adult Learning Boards will have a key role to play in ensuring a co-ordinated area-based input in respect of Adult Education into the strategic plans to be developed by the County/City Development Boards.

10.6 Staffing of VECs

The growth of activity under Adult Literacy and Adult Education generally, the expansion of the Back to Education Initiative, the development of supporting services such as guidance and childcare, the increase in youthwork activity, participation in Area-Based Partnerships, County/City Development Boards and the development of integrated approaches have all raised fundamental issues in relation to professional and administrative staffing levels in VECs. Needs in this area will be assessed as part of a comprehensive review which is to begin shortly.

Ultimately, for Local Adult Learning Boards to be effective, they will need to have access to a range of supports which include guidance, programme and staff development, technical support, literacy and community education facilitation staff, working in each area as part of an Adult Education team. This issue will be progressed in the light of the outcomes of the review mentioned above.

10.7 Monitoring and Evaluation

The developments outlined in this Paper will be subject to ongoing monitoring and evaluation through:-

- the social partnership fora and reporting arrangements underpinning the Programme for Prosperity and Fairness;

- the evaluation and monitoring arrangements governing the programmes set out in the *National Development Plan 2000 - 2006* and EU-aided Operational Programmes. These include formal six-monthly written progress reports, multi-agency monitoring committees, performance indicators setting out outputs and outcomes, and formal evaluation studies, thematic assessments, and mid-term and programmatic reviews;

- the work of the Department's Inspectorate in evaluating the quality and effectiveness of education services generally;

- the reporting and quality assurance processes of the various agencies and institutions which have a role in providing adult education or supporting services. A critical part of this process is the promotion across the system of a culture of team planning, self-appraisal, review and adaptation, under which the quality of education continues to evolve and improve on an ongoing basis in line with changing needs.

In addition, an over-arching evaluation study of developments and progress in promoting the Adult Education dimension of lifelong learning will be undertaken three years after the new structures proposed in this Chapter have been established. The study will also assess progress across all areas of the sector, including Further and Third-level education, quality assurance, staff development, certification and assessment, inter-agency linkages and structures, and development of supporting services.

10.8 Conclusion

Adult Education is the last area of mass education to be developed in Ireland. The rationale for investment in Adult Education does not rest on purely economic issues, but also on the central role of learning in creating a democratic society, in promoting culture and identity, and in enriching and strengthening individuals, families and communities.

Given the challenges which face our society in the new Millennium, it is vital that services for adult learners expand and evolve within an overall framework that ensures that lifelong learning becomes a reality. Achieving this goal will require concerted investment. It will also need cultural change, flexibility and responsiveness among existing institutions and providers, and a willingness to work in partnership with a wide range of interests. Many of the initial steps have already been taken in relation to literacy, second chance education, certification and assessment and programme support, and in securing a major increase in funds under the National Development Plan. This progress needs to be further built on, harnessing the expertise of the formal and non-formal sectors to work towards a lifelong learning vision for all.

The programme of change and development set out in this White Paper will be implemented on a phased basis in the light of the resources made available in the context of the National Development Plan and the annual Estimates for Public Servie provisions.

Appendices

Appendix 1

Quarterly National Household Survey (Quarter 2 1999)

FEMALE POPULATION 15-64, ESTIMATED BY HIGHEST EDUCATIONAL ATTAINMENT SEX AND ILO ECONOMIC STATUS, Q2 1999

FEMALE		AT WORK	UNEMP	NOT IN THE LABOUR FORCE	TOTAL
	AGE	THOU	THOU	THOU	THOU
01.Primary	15-24	5.4	1.6	37.1	44.1
	25-34	7.1	1.4	12.6	21.1
	35-44	14.2	2	24.1	40.3
	45-54	21.5	1.8	48.2	71.5
	55-64	11.1	0.8	61.3	73.3
	Total	59.3	7.6	183.3	250.2
02.Lower Secondary	15-24	25.2	4.1	71.2	100.5
	25-34	23.4	3.3	18.9	45.6
	35-44	26.5	2.3	26.2	55
	45-54	21.1	1.3	27.4	49.8
	55-64	6.9	0.3	19.7	26.9
	Total	103.1	11.3	163.4	277.8
03.Upper Secondary	15-24	57.3	4.5	52.6	114.4
	25-34	62.6	2.5	20.3	85.4
	35-44	47.6	1.5	28	77.1
	45-54	23.5	0.8	21.8	46.2
	55-64	7.6	0.2	17.1	25
	Total	198.7	9.7	139.8	348.1
04.Further Education/ Training	15-24	20.8	1.1	2.5	24.4
	25-34	33.8	1.2	7.4	42.4
	35-44	18.7	1.2	10.7	30.6
	45-54	10.1	0.4	7.3	17.8
	55-64	3.4	0.2	6.8	10.3
	Total	86.8	4.1	34.7	125.6
05.Third level non-degree	15-24	12.7	0.7	2.9	16.3
	25-34	25.7	0.7	3.6	29.9
	35-44	15.6	0.5	4.8	20.9
	45-54	10.2	0.5	3.4	14.1
	55-64	3.9	0.1	3.4	7.4
	Total	68.2	2.5	18	88.6

FEMALE		AT WORK	UNEMP	NOT IN THE LABOUR FORCE	TOTAL
	AGE	THOU	THOU	THOU	THOU
06.Degree or above	15-24	15.4	0.6	3.9	19.9
	25-34	42.1	0.7	4.4	47.1
	35-44	27.8	0.2	4.1	32.1
	45-54	15.5	0.1	3.6	19.2
	55-64	6	0.1	3.3	9.4
	Total	106.7	1.7	19.3	127.7
07.Other	15-24	0.9	0	1	1.9
	25-34	3	0.1	1.4	4.5
	35-44	2.5	0.2	0.9	3.6
	45-54	2	0	0.8	2.9
	55-64	0.8	0	0.6	1.4
	Total	9.2	0.4	4.6	14.3
08. Not Stated	15-24	0.9	0.1	0.5	1.5
	25-34	1.8	0	0.6	2.4
	35-44	1.2	0	0.6	1.8
	45-54	1	0	1.4	2.4
	55-64	0.4	0	1.4	1.8
	Total	5.3	0.1	4.4	9.9
TOTAL FEMALE		637.3	37.4	567.4	1242.2
Total Female Ages	15-24	138.6	12.7	171.7	323
	25-34	199.5	9.9	69.2	278.4
	35-44	154.1	7.9	99.4	261.4
	45-54	104.9	4.9	113.9	223.9
	55-64	40.1	1.7	113.6	155.5
TOTAL FEMALE		637.3	37.4	567.4	1242.2

Source: Quarterly National Household Survey,Q2 Mar-May 1999
Central Statistics Office, Cork

Quarterly National Household Survey (Quarter 2 1999)

MALE POPULATION 15-64, ESTIMATED BY HIGHEST EDUCATIONAL ATTAINMENT SEX AND ILO ECONOMIC STATUS, Q2 1999

MALE		AT WORK	UNEMP	NOT IN THE LABOUR FORCE	TOTAL
	AGE	THOU	THOU	THOU	THOU
01.Primary	15-24	9.1	3.7	40	52.9
	25-34	13.7	3.5	5.5	22.7
	35-44	27.5	5.6	8.5	41.7
	45-54	55.7	7.2	18	80.9
	55-64	44.6	2.9	33.8	81.3
	Total	150.7	22.8	105.8	279.4
02.Lower Secondary	15-24	45.4	5.8	64.6	115.9
	25-34	52.4	5	2.9	60.3
	35-44	59.3	4.2	3.8	67.3
	45-54	39.1	2.3	5.2	46.6
	55-64	14	0.4	7.3	21.7
	Total	210.2	17.8	83.8	311.7
03.Upper Secondary	15-24	73.6	4.4	39.5	117.5
	25-34	70.6	2.8	3.4	76.8
	35-44	57.6	2.1	2.5	62.3
	45-54	33.9	0.9	2.7	37.5
	55-64	12.4	0.2	5.9	18.5
	Total	248.1	10.5	54	312.6
04.Further Education/ Training	15-24	15.2	0.7	1.3	17.2
	25-34	35.4	1.2	0.6	37.2
	35-44	26.3	0.8	1.1	28.2
	45-54	19.2	0.9	1.2	21.3
	55-64	6.9	0.2	3.4	10.6
	Total	102.9	3.8	7.8	114.5
05.Third level Non-Degree	15-24	10.2	0.4	2.6	13.2
	25-34	23.7	0.5	1.1	25.3
	35-44	15.9	0.2	0.3	16.4
	45-54	8.9	0.2	0.5	9.6
	55-64	2.9	0.2	1.1	4.2
	Total	61.6	1.5	5.6	68.7

White Paper on Adult Education – Learning for Life

MALE		AT WORK	UNEMP	NOT IN THE LABOUR FORCE	TOTAL
	AGE	THOU	THOU	THOU	THOU
06.Degree or above	15-24	10.8	0.5	3.3	14.7
	25-34	44.6	0.7	2.5	47.9
	35-44	33.7	0.5	0.8	35
	45-54	25.3	0.2	0.9	26.4
	55-64	13.5	0.2	3.1	16.8
	Total	128.1	2.1	10.6	140.7
07.Other	15-24	1.1	0	0.8	2
	25-34	3.4	0.2	0.7	4.3
	35-44	3	0	0.2	3.2
	45-54	2	0.1	0.1	2.2
	55-64	1.4	0	0.7	2.1
	Total	10.8	0.4	2.5	13.7
08. Not Stated	15-24	1.2	0.1	0.4	1.6
	25-34	2	0.1	0.4	2.5
	35-44	2	0.1	0.3	2.3
	45-54	1.8	0.1	0.5	2.4
	55-64	0.8	0.1	0.5	1.4
	Total	7.7	0.5	2.1	10.3
TOTAL MALE		**920.1**	**59.3**	**272.1**	**1251.6**
Total Male Ages	**15-24**	**166.6**	**15.6**	**152.5**	**335**
	25-34	**245.8**	**14**	**17.1**	**277**
	35-44	**225.3**	**13.5**	**17.5**	**256.4**
	45-54	**185.9**	**11.9**	**29.1**	**226.9**
	55-64	**96.5**	**4.2**	**55.8**	**156.6**
TOTAL MALE		**920.1**	**59.2**	**272.1**	**1251.6**

Source: Quarterly National Household Survey,Q2 Mar-May 1999
Central Statistics Office, Cork

Appendix 2

Adult Community Education Network

Adult Literacy Organisers' Association

Age & Opportunity

Age Action Ireland Ltd.

AHEAD, Association for Higher Education Access & Disability

Annapurna Natural Healthcare

AONTAS, National Association of Adult Education

Area Development Management Ltd.

Arts Council, The

Association for Children & Adults with Learning Difficulties

Association of Chief Executive Officers of Vocational Education Committee

Association of Community & Comprehensive Schools

Association of Tutors & Trainers (Cork Social & Health Education Project Ltd)

Barry, Mr. John, Adult Education Organiser, Co. Longford VEC

BEAMS, Body Earth and Mind Soul, Holistic Therapy College, Castlebar

Bord na Gaeilge

Brogan, Ms. Veronica

CAFÉ, Creative Activity For Everyone

CERT, The State Tourism Training Agency

City of Dublin Vocational Education Committee

City of Galway Vocational Education Committee

Clare Co., Vocational Education Committee

Clondalkin Women's Network

Clondrinan Women's Network

CNEASTA, The Irish Council for Training, Development and Employment for Persons with Disabilities.

Coiste Comhairleach um Oideachas an Lucht Taistil

Combat Poverty Agency

Comdhail Náisiúnta na Gaeilge

Community Adult Learning Project, The

Community & Family Training Agency

Community Action Network Ltd.

Community Connections

Community Development & Leadership Training Courses

Community Women's Education Initiatives

Community Workers' Co-operative

Conference of Heads of Irish Universities

Conference of Religious of Ireland

Cork Combat Poverty Resource Project

Council of Directors of Institutes of Technology

Cross Border Women's Network

CVAF, Community and Voluntary Accreditation Forum

Department of Health and Children

Department of Social, Community & Family Affairs

Donegal, Co., Vocational Education Committee

Douglas Community School

Dowling, Ms. Catherine

Dublin Adult Learning Centre

Dublin City University

Dublin Co., Vocational Education Committee

Dublin Institute of Technology

Dun Laoghaire Institute of Art & Design

Dun Laoghaire Vocational Education Committee

Education Unit, The, Portlaoise Prison

EMPLOYMENT HORIZON

EMPLOYMENT INTEGRA

EMPLOYMENT NOW, New Opportunities for Women

FÁS

Fatima Community Centre

Federation of Irish Complementary Therapy Associations, The

Federation of Active Retirement Association

Fingal Further Education for Women, B. Brennan

Fingal Further Education for Women, Ms. Ann Broni, Vice Chairperson

Finglas/Cabra Partnership

Fitzgibbon, Mr. John

Flavin, Rev. Nicholas A.P., Co. Laois

FOROIGE, National Youth Development Organisation

FORUM, A rural development partnership in N.W. Connemara

Free University of Ireland

Galway County Libraries

Gardiner, Ms. Annette P

Geaney, Mr. Finbar

Giblin, Mr. Tom

Glancy, Mr. Christopher, Adult Education Organiser, Carlow

Gorey Community School

Goulding, Ms. Carole, Education Network

Hegarty, Ms. Mary Claire

Higher Education Equality Unit

Independent Radio & TV Commission

Information Society Commission

Institute of Guidance Counsellors

Irish Business and Employers' Confederation

Irish Countrywomen's Association

Irish Deaf Society

Irish Federation of University Teachers

Irish Institute of Training and Development, The

Irish Institute of Natural Therapy

Irish National Organisation of the Unemployed

Irish Reflexologists' Institute

Irish Rural Link

Irish Senior Citizens' Parliament

Irish Vocational Education Association

Kearns, Ms. Margaret

Kilkenny Co., Vocational Education Committee

Klear Ltd., Kilbarrack Local Education for Adult Renewal

Knocknacarra Active Retirement Association, The

Laois County Council

Learning Advisory Group Information Society Commission

Library Association of Ireland

Longford Irish Countrywomen's Association, (New Opportunities for Women) Ltd.

Madden, Ms. Mary, Aromatherapist

Mayo Co., Vocational Education Committee

McMenamin, Mary & Martin

Meath Co., Vocational Education Committee

Monaghan Co., Vocational Education Committee

MUINTEARAS, Togra Oideachais Gealtachta

Mulvihill, Mr. Paudie

Murray, Mr. Patrick

National Adult Literacy Agency

National Association for Deaf People

National Association of Community Education Directors

National Association of VTOS Co-ordinators

National Centre for Guidance in Education

National College of Art and Design

National College of Ireland

National Committee for Development in Education

National Consultative Committee on Racism and Interculturalism

National Council for Educational Awards

National Council for Vocational Awards

National Council on Ageing and Older People

National Distance Education Centre

National Traveller Women's Forum

White Paper on Adult Education – Learning for Life

National University of Ireland, Galway

National University of Ireland, Maynooth

National Women's Council of Ireland

National Youth Council of Ireland

Network of Adult & Continuing Educators

North East Access Radio

North West Inner City Women's Network

Northside Partnership

O'Hanlon, Mr. Alan, Adult Literacy Co-ordinator, Co. Meath VEC

O'Sullivan, Dr. Aine

Open University of Ireland, The

OSCAIL, National Distance Education Centre

Páirtíocht Ghaeltacht Thír Chonaill

Pavee Point Travellers' Centre

People's College, The

PLANET, The Network of Area- Based Partnerships

POWER Partnership

Ruhama Women's Project

Roscommon Co., Vocational Education Committee

Ruane, Mr. Michael,

Ryan, Ms. Mary

Secretariat of Secondary Schools

Senior Traveller Training Centres

Sinha, Shalini

Sligo, Co., Vocational Education Committee

Society of St. Vincent De Paul

South West Regional Authority

Southwest Kerry Women's Association

St. Patrick's College, Drumcondra

Tallaght Institute of Technology

Teachers' Union in Ireland

Teahan, Ms. Eileen

Tipperary Co., (North Riding) Vocational Education Committee

Tipperary, Co., (South Riding) Vocational Education Committee

Union of Students in Ireland

University College Dublin, NUI, Adult Education Office,

University College Dublin, NUI

University of Ulster, Professor Pauline Murphy

Vietnamese English Language Centre

Waterford Institute of Technology

WEI, Women's Education Initiative

WERRC, Women's Education Research and Resource Centre

West Limerick Women's Network

Westmeath Co., Vocational Education Committee

Wicklow Co., Vocational Education Committee

Women on Air

Women's Studies Steering Group, Mulhuddart, Co. Dublin

Worker's Educational Association Belfast

Working Class Access Network

Zena Project, Women's Education Initiative

Appendix 3

Oral Submissions on the Green Paper were received from the following Organisations

Age & Opportunity

AONTAS

Area Development Management

Arts Council

Association of Adult Education Organisers

Association of Adult Literacy Organisers

Association of Chief Executive Officers of Vocational Education Committees

Association of Community & Comprehensive Schools

Association of Co-ordinators of the Vocational Training Opportunities Scheme

Association of Secondary Teachers of Ireland

Bord na Gaeilge

CERT - The State Tourism Training Agency

CNEASTA – The Irish Council for Training, Development and Employment for Persons with Disabilities

Combat Poverty Agency

Comhdháil Náisiúnta na Gaeilge

Community Platform:

    Community Workers' Co-operative

    Conference of Religious of Ireland

    Forum for People with Disabilities

    Pavee Point

    Society of St. Vincent de Paul

Conference of Heads of Irish Universities

Conference of Religious of Ireland

Council of Directors of Institutes of Technology

Department of Tourism, Sport & Recreation

Dept. of An Taoiseach

Dept. of Arts, Heritage and the Gaeltacht

Dept. of Enterprise, Trade & Employment

Dept. of Justice, Equality & Law Reform:

     Asylum Section

     Equal Status Section

     Prison Education Service

     Probation and Welfare

Dept. of Social, Community & Family Affairs

FÁS

Federation of Irish Complementary Therapies Association

Forfás - Business Education & Training Partnership Forum

Higher Education Authority

Independent Radio and Television Commission

Information Society Commission

Irish Business and Employers' Confederation

Irish Congress of Trade Unions

Irish Countrywomen's Association

Irish Institute of Training and Development Ltd.

Irish National Organisation of Unemployed

Irish Refugee Council

Irish Rural Link

White Paper on Adult Education – Learning for Life

Irish Small & Medium Enterprises Association

Irish Traveller Movement

Irish Vocational Education Association

Joint Managerial Body

Library Council of Ireland

National Adult Literacy Association

National Association of Travellers' Training Centres

National Centre for Guidance in Education

National Consultative Committee on Racism

National Council for Educational Awards

National Council for Vocational Awards

National Economic and Social Council

National Parents' Council – Post Primary

National Rehabilitation Board

National Women's Council of Ireland

National Youth Council of Ireland

Open University

OSCAIL – National Distance Education Centre

PLANET – The Network of Area Based Partnerships

Refugee Language Support Unit

RTE – Radio Telefís Éireann

Strategy Group on Employment and Unemployment

Teachers' Union of Ireland

Teagasc

Údarás na Gaeltachta

Union of Students in Ireland

Women's Education Initiative:

ADAPT

Dublin Adult Learning Centre

Irish Deaf Society

Power Partnership

Shanty

Workers' Research Co-operative

Youthstart Guidance – NCGE

Bibliography

BIBLIOGRAPHY

An Chomhairle Leabharlanna (1999). *The Right to Read – the Development of Partnership Strategies for the Promotion of Literacy in the Community,* Dublin: The Library Council.

Arts Council (1999). *1999-2001: The Arts Plan,* Dublin: Stationery Office.

Callan, T., Layte, R., Nolan, B., Watson, D., Whelan, C.T., Williams, J. and Maitre, B. (1999). *Monitoring Poverty Trends,* Dublin: Stationery Office.

Central Statistics Office (1999). *Quarterly National Household Survey Q2,* Dublin: CSO.

Chamber of Commerce of Ireland (1999). *Labour Force, 1999,* Dublin: Chamber of Commerce of Ireland.

Clancy, P. (1999). "Participation of Mature Students in Higher Education in Ireland" in Fleming, T., Collins, T. and Coolahan, J. (eds.), *Higher Education : The Challenge of Lifelong Learning,* Maynooth: Centre for Educational Policy Studies, N.U.I. Maynooth.

> - (1995). *Interim Report of the Steering Committee's Technical Working Group,* Dublin: Higher Education Authority.

Commission on the Points System (1999). *Report of the Commission on the Points System,* Dublin: Stationery Office.

Conference of Religious of Ireland (1999). *Social Transformation and Lifelong Learning,* Dublin: CORI.

Davy Stockbrokers (2000). *The Irish Economic Report,* Dublin: Davy Stockbrokers.

Delors, J. (Chair) (1996). *Learning: The Treasure Within, Report to UNESCO of the International Commission on Education for the Twenty-First Century,* Paris: UNESCO.

Department of Education and Science (1999). *Ready to Learn : White Paper on Early Childhood Education*, Dublin: Stationery Office.

- (1999). *Report 2000 – The Women's Education Initiative*, Dublin: DES.

- (1999). *The New Deal: A Plan for Educational Opportunity*, Dublin: DES.

- (1998). *Green Paper on Adult Education: Adult Education in an Era of Lifelong Learning*, Dublin: Stationery Office.

- (1997). *International Adult Literacy Survey: Results for Ireland – Education 2000*, Dublin: Stationery Office.

- (1995). *Charting Our Education Future: White Paper on Education,* Dublin: Stationery Office.

Department for Education and Employment, (1998). *The Learning Age: A Renaissance for a New Britain*, London: HMSO.

Department of Education Northern Ireland, Training and Employment Agency (1999). *Lifelong Learning – A New Learning Culture for All*, Belfast: HMSO.

Department of Enterprise, Trade and Employment (1997). *White Paper on Human Resource Development*, Dublin: Stationery Office.

Department of the Environment and Local Government (2000). *Homelessness: An Integrated Strategy*, Dublin: Stationery Office.

Department of Public Enterprise (1998). *Report of the Advisory Committee on Telecommunications to the Minister for Public Enterprise*, Dublin: Stationery Office.

Department of Social, Community and Family Affairs (2000). *Report of the P2000 Working Group on Women's Access to Labour Market Opportunities*, Dublin: Stationery Office.

- (1997). *National Anti-Poverty Strategy, Sharing in Progress*, Dublin: Stationary Office

Economic and Social Research Institute (1998). *Annual School Leavers' Survey*, Dublin: ESRI.

Economic and Social Research Institute/FÁS (1998). *Manpower Forecasting Structures Report, No. 7 – Aspects of Occupational Change in the Irish Economy: Recent Trends and Future Prospects*, Dublin: FÁS.

Economic and Social Research Institute/Forfás (1999). *National Survey of Vacancies in the Private Non-Agricultural Sector 1998*, Dublin: ESRI.

Education Act, 1998.

European Commission (1996). *Strategy for Lifelong Learning*, Brussels: Office for Official Publications of the European Commission.

- (1995). *Teaching and Learning: Towards the Learning Society,* Brussels: Luxembourg: Office for Official Publications of the European Commission.

Expert Group on Future Skills Needs (1998). *Responding to Ireland's Growing Skill Needs: The First Report of the Expert Group on Future Skills Needs*, Dublin: Forfás.

- (2000). *Responding to Ireland's Growing Skill Needs: The Second Report of the Expert Group on Future Skills Needs*, Dublin: Forfás/FÁS.

Fitzgerald, G. (1999). "Lifelong Education" in Fleming, T., Collins, T. and Coolahan, J. (eds.), *Higher Education: The Challenge of Lifelong Learning*, Maynooth: Centre for Educational Policy Studies, N.U.I. Maynooth.

Goodbody Economic Consultants (1998). *The Disincentive Effects of Secondary Benefits*, Dublin: Goodbody Economic Consultants.

Government of Ireland (1999). *Ireland: National Development Plan, 2000-2006*, Dublin: Stationery Office.

    - (1998). *National Employment Action Plan, 1998*, Dublin: Stationery Office.

    - (1999). *National Employment Action Plan, 1999*, Dublin: Stationery Office.

    - (1999). *Implementing the Information Society in Ireland: An Action Plan*, Dublin: Stationery Office.

    - (2000). *National Employment Action Plan, 2000*, Dublin: Stationery Office.

    - (2000). *Programme for Prosperity and Fairness*, Dublin: Stationery Office.

Higher Education Authority (1999). *Report of Review Committee on Post Secondary Education and Training Places*, Dublin: HEA.

Higher Education Equality Unit (1999). *Doing It Differently – Addressing Racism and Discrimination against Members of Minority Ethnic Groups in Higher Education in Ireland*, Cork: HEEU.

Information Society Ireland (1999). *Building a Capacity for Change: Lifelong Learning in the Information Society*, Dublin: Stationery Office.

Irish Vocational Education Association (1999). *Pathways to Progress: An IVEA Submission in Response to the Green Paper on Adult Education*, Dublin: IVEA.

Kenny, I. (1983). *Report of the Commission on Adult Education*, Dublin: Stationery Office.

Lennon, N. (1999). *Towards An Integrated Accreditation Framework*, Dublin: Community and Voluntary Accreditation Forum.

Library Association of Ireland (1999). *Public Libraries 2000: National Network – Local Service*, Dublin: Library Association of Ireland.

Longworth, N. and Davies, W.K. (1996). *Lifelong Learning: New Vision, New Implications, New Roles for People, Organisations, Nations and Communities in the 21st century*, London: Kogan Page.

Lynch, K. (1999). *Equality in Education*, Dublin: Gill & Macmillan.

Lynch, K., Brannick, T., Clancy, P. and Drudy, S. (1999). *Points and Performance in Higher Education: A Study of the Predictive Validity of the Points System, Research Paper No.4*, Dublin: Stationery Office.

McNamara, G. (1998). *Guidance in Adult and Continuing Education*, Dublin: National Centre for Guidance in Education.

Murphy, C. (1973). *Adult Education in Ireland: A Report of a Committee Appointed by the Minister for Education*, Dublin: Stationery Office.

National Competitiveness Council (1999). *Annual Competitiveness Report 1999*, Dublin: Forfás.

National Economic and Social Council (1999). *Opportunities, Challenges and Capacities for Choice*, Dublin: NESC.

OECD (1997). *"Literacy Skills for the Knowledge Society" in International Adult Literacy Survey*, Paris: OECD.

- (1995). *Economic Survey of Ireland, 1995*, Paris: OECD.

- (1996). *Lifelong Learning for All,* Paris: OECD.

- (1997). *Education at a Glance: Policy Analysis*, Paris: OECD.

- (1998). *Education at a Glance: Policy Analysis* Paris: OECD.

- (1998). *Education Policy Analysis*, Paris: OECD.

- (1999). *Economic Survey of Ireland, 1999*, Paris: OECD.

- (2000). *Education at a Glance: OECD Indicators 2000*, Paris: OECD.

Ó Murchú, M.W. (1973). *Adult Education in Ireland*, Prague: European Centre for Leisure and Education.

Qualifications (Education and Training) Act, 1999.

Ruane, F.P. and Sutherland, J.M. (1999). *Women in the Labour Force*, Dublin: Employment Equality Agency.

Ryan, A.B. and Collins. T. (1999). *ASTI-JMB Pilot Project in Adult Education - Evaluation Report*, Maynooth: (Unpublished).

Sabel, C. (1996). *Ireland: Local Partnerships and Social Innovation*, Paris: OECD.

Smyth, A. (1999) in McCann, C. *A Study of Feminist Education as an Empowerment Strategy for Community Based Women's Groups in Ireland*, Dublin: WERRC.

Vocational Education Act, 1930.

Wagner, A. (1999). "Lifelong Learning and Higher Education: The International Context" in Fleming, T., Collins, T. and Coolahan, J. (eds.), *Higher Education: The Challenge of Lifelong Learning*, Maynooth: Centre for Educational Policy Studies, N.U.I. Maynooth.

Warner, K. (1993). *Working through an Adult Education Model: Prison Education in Ireland*, Dublin: Prisons Office.

Waterford Institute of Technology (1999). *Looking for Something in the Dark: Educational Guidance Provision for Adults*, Integra: A New Start Project, WIT.

Leabharlann Chill Mhantáin

3 0006 00152644 2